SCIENCE AND THE
NEW AGE CHALLENGE

SCIENCE AND THE NEW AGE CHALLENGE

Ernest Lucas

APOLLOS (an imprint of Inter-Varsity Press),
38 De Montfort Street, Leicester LE1 7GP

First published 1996

British Library Cataloguing in Publication Data
A catalogue record for this book is available from the British Library.

ISBN 0–85111–440–7

Set in Palatino
Photoset by Parker Typesetting Service, Leicester
Printed in Great Britain by Clays Ltd, Bungay, Suffolk

Inter-Varsity Press is the book-publishing division of the Universities and
Colleges Christian Fellowship (formerly the Inter-Varsity Fellowship), a
student movement linking Christian Unions in universities and colleges
throughout the United Kingdom and the Republic of Ireland, and a member
movement of the International Fellowship of Evangelical Students.
For information about local and national activities write to UCCF,
38 De Montfort Street, Leicester LE1 7GP.

Dedication

This book is dedicated to the students and staff of the Institute for Contemporary Christianity, St Peter's Church, Vere Street, London, 1986–1994. It was the students at the Institute who prompted me to study the New Age movement by their questions about it. They then sharpened my thinking about it in the discussions which followed lectures which I gave on the basis of my researches.

Acknowledgment

The material in chapters 1 to 4 is based on two papers which were published in 1992 in the journal *Science and Christian Belief*, vol. 4.1, for which the author was given an award under the John Templeton Foundation's Humility Theology Program.

CONTENTS

INTRODUCTION

Over the last five years or so, I have watched a change taking place in two or three large academic bookshops which I frequent. The stock of books in their Theology section has shrunk and a new section has grown to equal or surpass it in size, labelled 'Esoterica' or 'New Age'. This is a symptom of a wider social phenomenon.

When I began working at the Institute for Contemporary Christianity in London in 1986, the term 'New Age' was virtually unheard of in the UK. The Institute draws students from all over the world, and it was students from North America and Scandinavia who first drew the phenomenon to my attention and prompted me to find out more about it. I knew that the New Age had well and truly arrived in the UK when, one morning in July 1990, one of the 'freebie' magazines offered to commuters as we left Charing Cross station carried the cover story, 'New Age Faith – What's in it for You?'

Early in my attempt to understand the New Age I read some of the autobiographies of Shirley MacLaine. What particularly caught my attention was the fact that, on a number of occasions, she claimed that modern science was providing support for the kind of ideas that she had discovered in her New Age faith. Her books lack footnotes so I had to go on a hunt to track down the sources of her claims. I found them in the writings of some of the people whose work I discuss in this book. Significantly, they are writers whose books appear in both the Esoterica and the Science sections of the bookshops I mentioned –

11

another symptom of what is going on more widely.

Although my main field of work is now Biblical Studies, I write this book primarily as a scientist. I worked for seven years in chemical and biochemical research, and still find science fascinating in all its branches – from particle physics to cosmology, and from molecular biology to ecology. As I have studied the interaction between science and New Age thought, three convictions have developed. The first is that the appeal made to science by many New Agers is sincere but superficial. It is generally made at second hand, relying on those scientists who have written about the subject. This brings me to my second conviction, that the arguments used by these scientists are on the whole muddled and mistaken. It frequently happens that, when scientists try to draw out philosophical and religious implications from science, their thinking seems to lose the sharpness it has when they are doing science itself. They make various illegitimate jumps from 'physics' (in its old sense of the study of nature) to metaphysics. My third conviction is that an orthodox Christian world-view provides the most satisfactory framework for doing science and for integrating 'physics' with metaphysics.

This book concentrates on the first two convictions, because I know of no other book that deals with these matters in detail. There are a number of good books[1] which discuss the interaction between science and Christianity, and so I do not deal with this in detail. Because the book is dealing with science-based claims, and also to keep it to a reasonable length, I concentrate on a scientific critique of these claims. While I do express my Christian response to the issues raised, there are fuller Christian treatments of many of these already in print, as the Notes indicate.

For the sake of those who are still unsure what is meant by the New Age movement, the book begins with a brief introduction and overview of this phenomenon. Chapter 2 introduces the subject of the book, the paradoxical claim that some New Age writers make that science supports their view of reality. The book then looks in detail at that claim with regard to three main areas of science: physics (chapters 3 and 4), biology (chapters 5 to 8) and ecology (chapters 9 to 11). The final chapter draws together my conclusions.

1

WHAT IS THE NEW AGE MOVEMENT?

The New Age movement is not a unified movement or an organized conspiracy.[1] It is a melting-pot of ideas, with many forms and faces. The common factor is a reaction against the spiritual aridity of the secularism which now dominates Western culture. Elliot Miller says of it:

> The new Age Movement then is an extremely large, *loosely* structured network of organizations and individuals bound together by common values (based in mysticism and monism – the world view that 'all is one') and a common vision (a coming 'new age' of peace and mass enlightenment, the 'Age of Aquarius').[2]

In many cases there is a conscious rejection of orthodox Christianity. Douglas Groothuis describes it as

> . . . a smorgasbord of spiritual substitutes for Christianity, all heralding our unlimited potential to transform ourselves and the planet so that a 'New Age of peace, light and love' will break forth.[3]

Its roots

Although in one sense a phenomenon of the late 1980s, the New Age movement has quite deep roots.

Sociologically it is an outgrowth of the counter-culture movements of the 1960s. Miller lists five features of these movements which are also found in the New Age movement: anti-materialism, attempts to build alternative communities, an exaltation of nature, a rejection of traditional morality, and a fascination with the occult.[4] While the 60s movements were largely student-led youth movements, however, the New Age movement appeals to a much wider age range, and its leading personalities are on the whole people from the world of the media rather the universities.

Spiritually its roots are in the religions of the East. In particular the New Age movement can be seen as picking up the baton of the westernized version of Eastern religions which gained some popularity in the second half of the nineteenth century, as epitomized by the Theosophical Society and its off-shoots.

The occult element in the movement is most obvious in the forms of astrology and mediumship ('channelling', as New Agers call it). The idea of a new age has its origins in astrology. In astrology the position of the Sun against the background stellar constellations at the time of the Spring Equinox is of great significance. The Spring Equinox is the time when day and night are of equal length (March 20th or 21st). For the last 2,000 years or so the Sun has been in the constellation of Pisces (the Fishes) at this time. According to most astrologers, in the later part of the twentieth century it began to move into Aquarius (The Water Bearer), though there are different views of the exact date of the transition.[5] Astrologers claim that this transition heralds a change in the dominant spiritual influence in the world from Christianity (associated since early Christian times with the symbol of a fish) to the rise of a new, more universal spirituality. Incidentally, this is a very Western-centred view of the world's spiritual history. One can hardly say that Christianity has been the dominant spiritual influence in India and Asia for the last 2,000 years!

Foundation principles

Despite the complexity of the New Age movement, there do seem to be some basic ideas that are widely held by those who identify themselves as New Agers. These ideas are drawn largely from Eastern religions but the influence of Western secular humanism has left its mark also. They can be summed up in four words.

1. Monism

Monism is the belief that 'all is one', that everything is part of one, single, undifferentiated ultimate reality. The tendency among New Agers is to stress that all is consciousness and that there is a single, unified consciousness. Individuals are fragments of this oneness. Fritjof Capra says, 'All individuality dissolves into universal, undifferentiated oneness in the ultimate state of consciousness.'[6]

The differences which we perceive and think are real (*e.g.* that I seem to be distinct from someone else) are the result of ignorant, unenlightened attitudes.

2. Pantheism

Pantheism is the belief that 'all is God'. This means that everything is a manifestation of God. Each individual is innately divine. Shirley MacLaine says that *the* giant truth of the New Age movement is

> . . . that the one individual is his or her own best teacher, and that no other idol or false image should be worshipped or adored because the God we are all seeking lies inside oneself, not outside.[7]

Eileen Caddy, one of the founders of the Findhorn Community, gives the following 'channelled' message:

> I AM THAT I AM. I AM the alpha and omega and all life. Rejoice, My beloveds, for you are all part of the glorious wholeness, all part of that glorious oneness.[8]

15

3. *Autonomy*

The total freedom or autonomy of human beings is believed in on the grounds that each one is part of the divine essence. Put crudely, this is the view that 'since I am God, who can push me around?' This leads to a stress on 'doing your own thing'. As Jack Underhill puts it:

> You are the only thing that is real . . . Accept that and then take the responsibility for making your own life what you want it to be.[9]

This stress on the autonomy of the individual stands in contrast to the conclusion which classical Eastern religions draw from monistic pantheism. They stress the need to lose one's sense of individuality and the personal desires that go with it, in order to realize one's unity with the ultimate reality. The fact that New Age thinking does not follow that route reflects the strong individualism inherent in Western secular humanism, from which the New Agers have not fully freed themselves.

4. *Relativism*

If all the differences in this life are unreal, then there is no place for dogmatism. The concepts of absolute good or evil, or truth and falsehood, are meaningless if all is one and all is God. As Carol Riddell puts it:

> There is only one God, only the 'Atma' or Essence. Everything that seems otherwise is the result of the way it is viewed, not its reality. The notions of evil and sin and their accompanying feelings of guilt have led to a widespread sense of inadequacy and worthlessness, especially among some Christians. But ultimate Good is not a quality that can be defined by its relationship to that which is perceived as not-good, its negation. It is, simply, the truth, that which *is*. The opposite of that which is, is that which *is not*, i.e. non-existence. There is therefore only Good, and its discovery is the discovery of truth. That which is not good, which is evil, is not something different from God – an alternative, inherently evil universal force – but behaviour without knowledge of the truth.[10]

Manifestations of the New Age

Sincerely held beliefs affect behaviour. This is as true of New Agers as it is of Christians. This can be seen in the activities and organizations which attract the interest and support of New Agers.

1. Monism and international peace movements

Monism leads to support for international peace movements. Since 'all is one', New Agers believe that we are evolving spiritually and socially towards a single, united humanity. This they call the 'planetization' of human society. As a result they are very willing to give moral, and sometimes active, support to the United Nations and other international organizations, especially those which work for peace. There are also specifically New Age pressure groups such as Planetary Citizens and World Goodwill. Monism also encourages support for environmental groups such as Greenpeace, the World Wide Fund for Nature and the green political parties. This follows naturally from the belief that the non-human world is as much part of the ultimate undifferentiated oneness as are humans. Therefore the unity of existing ecosystems is to be restored or preserved.

2. Pantheism and the coming together of religions

With its belief that 'all is God', pantheism leads naturally to the belief that all religions are but different ways to the same ultimate divine reality. As Carol Riddell puts it:

> If God is the Indweller, the reality in us all, then how we seek to discover Him is a matter of cultural background, or personal choice. Our job is to find the means of Self-discovery that best leads us forward from our present starting point . . . We can no longer judge other cultures or religions either better or worse than our own.[11]

This leads to involvement in various inter-faith events and organizations which work for or express the coming together of different religions. Because the divine is also present in the non-human world, it has also encouraged a revival of animistic religions, which see spirits or spiritual forces at work in natural objects and events. Some New Agers are therefore very interested in the pre-Christian pagan religions of Europe, such as Celtic Druidism and the old Norse religions. In North America it leads to an interest in the religions of the indigenous peoples. Closely related to this is an interest in various forms of magic which claim to harness natural forces for spiritual ends.

3. Autonomy and the human potential movement

Autonomy leads to involvement in the human potential movement in its many forms. This movement has roots that pre-date the New Age movement but fit in well with its belief in the inherent divinity of the individual. If that divinity can be harnessed then one's potential is limitless. One common expression of this belief is in the technique of creative visualization. This seeks to use the power of our imagination to bring about changes in physical reality, in us or in the world around us. Melita Denning writes:

> Truly by the power of this source channelled through the conscious and unconscious levels of your own psyche, the action takes place on the corresponding levels of the external universe, to bring about the presentation to you on the earthly level of what you have imaged. This is WHY you can truly affirm that what you visualize IS YOURS NOW.[12]

In particular, New Age ideology and techniques have been incorporated into business management training programmes that have been widely marketed. These include EST (Erhard Seminar Training), Silva Mind Control, Lifespring, and Results Partnership courses.

It is important for Christians to avoid both paranoia and naïvety about the New Age movement. It is paranoic to label, say, all international peace organizations or green movements 'New Age' and shun them just because they attract New Agers. There is good reason for them to attract Christians too! Constructive Christian involvement in such areas is the best response to make to the New Age movement. It would be naïve to ignore the fact that New Age groups are working in peace organizations or green movements. Similarly, when people are attracted to an organization because of its stated aims, it it often not until they are quite involved that it is made clear to them that the organization works on the basis of New Age ideology.

The New Age and salvation

The New Age movement has a definite message of salvation for a world that is clearly in a mess. What is needed, and is offered, is transformation for both the individual and the planet. That is why Marilyn Ferguson's manifesto for the New Age movement was subtitled 'Personal and Social Transformation in the 1980s'.[13]

For the New Agers that root problem is essentially intellectual, not moral. This is made clear in the quotation from Carol Riddell already given (when we discussed relativism as a feature of the movement, on page 16):

> That which is not good, which is evil, is not something different from God – an alternative, inherently evil universal force – but behaviour without knowledge of the truth.

Our crises come from our blindness to our innate divinity and oneness. If only we could understand and accept these, all would be well. What is needed is personal transformation. This will happen when we actualize (make real) our divine nature. To quote Riddell again:

> In the search for spirit, the meaning of life is twofold. Firstly, we are trying to discover who we really are – to experience the Divine within. Secondly, we are trying to express what we discover, through our actions in the perceived world. People who are adopting this twofold path as their purpose in life are transcending the stage 'Home sapiens', and are the early representatives of a new human development – 'Homo divinus'. The expanded consciousness of 'Homo divinus' will enable us to resolve the problems of our current civilization.[14]

How are we to 'discover who we really are' and to actualize our divinity? Scanning the New Age literature one finds claims that actualization can be brought about by many different means: meditation (transcendental meditation, yoga); positive thinking (the human potential movement); music; the occult (channelling, magic); and mind-changing drugs.

The common factor in all these approaches is that they have the potential to enable one to experience an altered state of consciousness (ASC) in which there is the experience of oneness with ultimate reality. Meditation, in various forms, is the classic way of doing this. This often involves the use of a 'mantra', a word or phrase on which the meditator concentrates and repeats time and again. This technique clears the mind of all other thoughts and, eventually, one may flip over into an ASC. Much positive thinking seems to be a form of self-hypnosis, often using the repetition of slogans (*e.g.* 'I am great, I really am'), and so can be a way of achieving as ASC. Genuine New Age music (there is now a great deal which is little more than a cashing-in on a lucrative market) has a simple, repetitive melody and rhythm. It is intended as an aid to meditation, and so basically provides a melodic mantra which can promote the flip over into an ASC. The occult approach makes use of the trance state to get in touch with spiritual forces or beings. Mind-changing drugs provide the quick fix of using chemicals to achieve an ASC. Many New Agers are wary of the use of drugs, recognizing that they damage both the body and the mind. Given their relativistic outlook, however, it is hard for them to say that drug use is 'wrong'. The great variety of approaches to ASCs is a good example of the smorgasbord nature of the movement. If one approach does not work for you, you can move on to another.

Many New Agers accept the Hindu doctrine of reincarnation and the law of karma. Reincarnation is the belief that instead of just one life, we have a series of lives. The 'law of karma' says that how we live in this life determines our experiences in the next life. These doctrines expand the time scale for actualization to take place. You may not achieve it in this life, but the progress you make can give you a flying start in the next.

Some New Agers seem to be concerned only with their own personal spiritual transformation. Shirley MacLaine, once a political activist, describes a change in her attitude following her immersion in the New Age movement:

The individual identity was what interested me. And so, although there was still much I agreed with and was attracted to within the sociopolitical activism of the time, I fundamentally understood that the only change I could really effect was the change within myself. That was where I would grow and progress to more understanding. So I began to veer away from political and social movements.[15]

This is not total solipsism. On one occasion she took as her New Year's resolution 'to improve myself – which would in turn improve the world I lived in'.[16] Behind this is the belief that personal transformation will lead to global transformation once enough people have undergone personal transformation. This rests on the theory of a 'critical mass' of new consciousness. As Mark Satin puts it:

> A critical mass is the number of concerned and committed people it would take to move the continent – democratically – in a New Age direction.[17]

Satin goes on to say that estimates of this 'critical mass' range from 2% to 20% of the population. There is also a difference in opinion over how this critical mass should operate. For some, all that is needed is cultivation of one's personal spirituality. Others favour such corporate spiritual means as mass meetings for transcendental meditation to radiate peace and harmony out into the world. There are also those who favour political activism by individuals and by pressure groups.

Although many New Agers are antagonistic to Christianity, or ignore it as *passé*, some want to claim that Jesus is on their side. They present him as an outstanding spiritual master and teacher who was illumined by the universal 'Christ spirit', which can illumine us all. His importance is that he shows how we can all become 'christs'. Riddell reinterprets New Testament teaching in this way:

> The 'second coming' is the availability to all, on a global basis, of the consciousness of Christ, rather than a new physical appearance of his body. By crucifying the ego of our materialistic desires, we can be resurrected into the Christ consciousness of the true meaning of life, and live in happiness and harmony together.[18]

Christ is said to have gained much of this spiritual wisdom from travelling in India and Tibet to study the Eastern religions there. He taught the doctrines of reincarnation and karma, which were removed from the New Testament by the leaders of the early church. His death was that of a religious martyr who was ahead of his time, not an atoning sacrifice.[19]

The New Age and truth

New Agers are critical of Enlightenment rationalism and its distinction between subject and object. For them truth transcends the true/false distinctions of traditional Western logic (see page 16 above regarding relativism). It is subjective rather than objective, a matter of feelings as much as, if not more than, reasoning. This makes it possible to hold apparently contradictory beliefs. In the area of spirituality in particular, rationality has no place. One simply has to experience the truth to 'feel' that it is right. As one of Shirley MacLaine's spirit guides told her:

> The path to inner peace is not through the intellect but through the inner heart. Within the inner heart one finds God, peace and oneself. Intellectual sceptics avoid themselves. The *self*, however, knows the divine truth because the self is itself Divine.[20]

2

SCIENCE AND KNOWLEDGE IN THE NEW AGE

In a book which tries to put the current New Age movement into a broad historical context of groups which have claimed to herald the arrival of heaven on earth, Rachel Storm describes the movement as

> . . . a vast umbrella movement embracing countless groups, gurus and individuals, bound together by a belief that the world is undergoing a transformation or shift in consciousness which will usher in a new mode of being, an earthly paradise . . . By dismissing logical argument, by putting intuition above intellect and feeling above theory, the New Age happily embraces wildly differing creeds. For the New Age is not 'either/or' but 'both/and', as its proponents so often insist.[1]

For the average scientist the approach to truth implied here is, to say the least, worrying. Modern science seems to have progressed by making either/or distinctions: either the Sun and the planets revolve around the Earth, or the Earth and the planets revolve around the Sun; either substances burning in air lose phlogiston or they combine with oxygen; biological change is due either to the inheritance of acquired characteristics or to genetic mutation. Moreover, logical argument has been taken to be central to the scientific method:

The scientific community sees itself as the very paradigm of institutional-ized rationality. It is taken to be in possession of something, the scientific method, which generates a 'logic of justification'. That is, it provides a technique for the objective appraisal of the merits of scientific theories. In addition it has even been claimed by some that the scientific method includes a 'logic of discovery', which is to say that it provides devices to assist the scientist in the discovery of new theories.[2]

Some recent historians, sociologists and philosophers of science, most notably perhaps Feyerabend[3] and Kuhn,[4] have attacked this rational view of science. However, by and large both the philosophers and practitioners of science more or less accept it. Clearly, intuition has its place in the practice of science, but it has to come under the discipline of the intellect. Personal feelings have to give way to the goal of dispassionate objectivity in the search for truth.

Right brain, left brain

If New Agers regard the Buddha and Jesus as incarnations of the 'Christ spirit', then a prime candidate for an incarnation of the 'anti-Christ spirit' (if such a thing can exist in a monistic universe) must be the seventeenth-century Frenchman René Descartes, the philosopher whom New Agers love to hate. This is because he is seen as the father of modern rationalism. He argued that certainty is to be achieved by deductive reasoning from self-evident truths or innate ideas. Following the rise of empiricism, the belief that sense experience is a reliable source and basis for what we can know, Descartes's 'self-evident truths' became, for many people, what scientists discovered by their investigation of the physical world. As a result scientific knowledge is widely viewed, at least in Western culture, as 'the truth'. As Theodore Roszak put it:

> What is 'reliable knowledge'? How do we know it when we see it? The answer is: reliable knowledge is knowledge that is scientifically sound, since science is that to which modern man refers for the definitive explication of reality.[5]

This view of 'reliable knowledge' banishes into limbo large areas of human experience, such as aesthetics, morals and religion. What status are we to give to these? In practice in Western culture they have been marginalized and belittled. This has led to a spiritual aridity in the culture, against which New Agers are protesting. One form that this protest takes is a rejection of reason as the only, or primary, means of discovering truth.

Some New Agers go to the extreme of trying to deny reason any legitimate place within New Age thought. Bhagwan Shree Rajneesh, who is a guru to some New Agers, asserts:

> It is not that the intellect sometimes misunderstands. Rather, the intellect always misunderstands. It is not that the intellect sometimes errs; it is that the intellect is the error. It always errs.[6]

Most New Agers, however, do not go to that extreme. They prefer to present rational and non-rational mental processes as complementary, though it must be said that preference often seems to be given to the non-rational. A common way of expressing this complementarity, which gives it a quasi-scientific validity (which is useful when trying to commend the idea to those for whom scientific knowledge is 'reliable truth'), is by means of Robert Ornstein's theory of brain hemispheres.[7] This began as a psychological theory based on the behaviour of patients who, in the 1960s and 1970s, underwent brain surgery for the treatment of severe epilepsy. The brain consists of two hemispheres, a right and a left one, connected by a bundle of fibres called the corpus callosum. In these patients the corpus callosum was cut, resulting in a 'split brain'. It was found that the two hemispheres functioned separately and were responsible for different activities. The right hemisphere controls the motion on the left side of the body and the left that on the right side. The left hemisphere seems to control speech, whereas the right is important for visual functions, such as understanding spatial relationships.

The experiments involving split-brain subjects suggest that the different specializations of the two hemispheres of the brain represent preferences rather than absolute distinctions in function.[8] However, a general theory, which goes well beyond the actual evidence, has been constructed and is widely used by New Agers. This regards the 'left brain', with its control of speech, as the seat of our rational, analytical and systematizing powers. Conversely the 'right brain' is regarded as the seat of our emotions, intuition, sexuality and creativity.

The functions attributed to the left brain are those which Western society has traditionally associated with the male, high culture and all that is finest in us. The functions of the right brain correspond to what Western society has tended to dismiss as feminine and irrational. New Agers diagnose the root cause of many of our society's problems as being an excessive reliance on the left brain. Marilyn Ferguson puts it starkly:

> Without the benefit of a scalpel, we perform split-brain surgery on ourselves. We isolate heart and mind. Cut off from the fantasy, dreams, intuitions and holistic processes of the right brain, the left is sterile. And the right brain, cut off from integration with its organizing partner, keeps recycling its emotional charge. Feelings are dammed, perhaps to work private mischief in fatigue, illness, neurosis, a pervasive sense of something wrong, something missing – a kind of cosmic homesickness. This fragmentation costs us our health and our capacity for intimacy . . . it also costs us our ability to learn, create, innovate.[9]

It follows from this that what we need to do is to develop techniques which are

> . . . designed to reopen the bridge between the right and left to through traffic, to increase the left brain's awareness of its counterpart . . . Whatever lowers the barrier and lets the unclaimed material emerge is transformative . . . Incantations, mantras, poetry, and secret sacred words are all bridges that join the two brains.[10]

It is on this basis that New Agers insist that intuition, feeling and ASCs (altered states of consciousness) are all valid ways of knowing. They are ways of obtaining knowledge about reality. Indeed, the tendency is to see them as superior ways to knowledge. The left-brain empirical method that relies on sensory perception and the use of reason provides us with more or less reliable knowledge about the world of appearances. The right-brain approaches, however, enable us to experience the reality which lies behind the world of appearances. This is what Fritjof Capra calls 'absolute knowledge:

> Absolute knowledge is thus an entirely non-intellectual experience of reality, an experience arising in a non-ordinary state of consciousness which may be called a 'meditative' or mystical state.[11]

There is, of course, a natural tendency to give a higher status to such absolute knowledge of reality-as-it-is behind the world of appearances than to the more limited knowledge of the world of appearances provided by the empirical approach of science. At this point it is worth noting how 'channelled' knowledge fits into the New Age scheme of things. It comes from contact with spirits, disembodied entities who, it is assumed, must know more about reality than we do because they live in the 'spiritual' dimension. They can communicate with us using human channels or mediums. Information gained this way is regarded by many New Agers as just as reliable as any other.

With this background of the New Age approach to knowledge and how we know things, we can now turn specifically to the New Age understanding and critique of science.

The New Age criticism of the scientific method

Capra provides a clear and succinct exposition of the New Age criticism of the scientific method.[12] He links the criticism with four of the founding fathers of modern science. We will follow his approach without entering into any debate about how accurately he represents the actual thinking of the people concerned and their role in the development of science.

Galileo postulated that scientists should restrict themselves to studying the essential properties of material bodies (shapes, numbers and movement) which could be measured and quantified. This was because these properties can be expressed in the language of mathematics, which he regarded as the 'language' in which the 'book of nature' is written. He regarded other properties (such as colour, taste and smell) as subjective mental projections which should be excluded from the domain of science. Capra accepts that Galileo's strategy has been extremely successful. However, he criticizes it because it removes from the realm of scientific discourse aesthetics, ethical sensibility, feelings, motives, intentions, soul, consciousness and spirit; in other words, 'experience as such'. Thanks to Galileo, scientists became obsessed with measurement and quantification, and this eventually brought about a great change in the way reality was understood.

Bacon was the first to formulate a clear theory of inductive procedure, *i.e.* the making of experiments in order to draw general conclusions from them, which were then to be tested by further experiments. Capra criticizes Bacon for his strong, and successful, support of the view that the goal of science is knowledge that can be used to dominate and control nature. This banished the ancient wisdom, which wanted to understand the natural order so as to live in harmony with it. The ecological problems posed by science and technology flow from this 'Baconian spirit'.

Descartes comes in for threefold criticism. First, he is taken to task for believing that 'all science is certain, evident knowledge'. Capra asserts that twentieth-century physics has shown 'very forcefully' that there is no absolute truth in science. Despite this, the Cartesian belief in scientific truth is still widespread today and is reflected in the scientism that has become typical of Western culture. Secondly, Capra criticizes Descartes's analytic method of reasoning. This consisted in breaking up thoughts and problems into pieces and then arranging these in their logical order. He admits that this has 'proved extremely useful' in the development of science and technology, but he objects to its outcome – reductionism, *i.e.* the belief that all aspects of complex problems can be understood by reducing them to their constituent parts. Thirdly, Capra is critical of Descartes's sharp distinction between mind and matter. This arose from Descartes's application of the method of radical doubt, which led him to the conclusion that the one thing he could not doubt was his existence as a thinker. Hence his celebrated statement, *'Cogito ergo sum'*, 'I am thinking, therefore I exist.' This made mind more certain for him than matter, and led him to the conclusion that the two were separate and fundamentally different. Mind was associated with the thinking, experiencing 'I', whereas matter was seen as nothing but a machine. Non-human nature works according to mechanical laws, which can be expressed in mathematics. This produced a drastic change in people's image of nature and their attitude towards it. This change laid nature open to the manipulation and exploitation that have become typical of Western culture.

Newton is credited with combining the empirical, inductive approach of Bacon with Descartes's rational, deductive method to produce 'the methodology upon which natural science has been based ever since'. He promulgated the view that all physical phenomena are the result of the motion of material particles within absolute space and time. That motion is governed by fixed laws. The result was a view of nature as a giant cosmic machine, completely causal and determinate. This picture of a perfect world machine, says Capra,

> . . . implied an external creator; a monarchical god who ruled the world from above by imposing his divine law on it. The physical phenomena themselves were not thought to be divine in any sense, and when science made it more and more difficult to believe in such a god, the divine disappeared completely from the scientific world view, leaving behind the spiritual vacuum that has become characteristic of the mainstream of our culture. The philosophical basis of this secularization of nature was the Cartesian division between spirit and matter. As a consequence of this division, the world was believed to be a mechanical system that could be described objectively, without ever mentioning the human observer, and such an objective description of nature became the ideal of all science.[13]

In this critique we find a catalogue of those things which inspire antipathy in New Agers in general: reductionism; a mechanistic, deterministic view of the universe; the valuing of rationality above intuition or feeling; the divorce between mind or consciousness and matter; the idea of objective truth; and a materialism which ignores the spiritual aspect of reality.

The New Age attitude to science

Given the apparent total opposition between the approaches to knowledge and truth of New Age and scientific thinking, it is not surprising that many proponents of the New Age are highly critical of science. Capra comments:

> In our Western culture, which is still dominated by the mechanistic, fragmented view of the world, an increasing number of people have seen this as the underlying reason for the widespread dissatisfaction in our society, and many have turned to Eastern ways of liberation. It is interesting, and perhaps not too surprising, that those who are attracted by Eastern mysticism, who consult the *I Ching* and practise Yoga or other forms of meditation, in general have a marked anti-scientific attitude. They tend to see science, and physics in particular, as an unimaginative, narrow-minded discipline which is responsible for all the evils of modern technology.[14]

It would seem reasonable to conclude that if New Age thinking becomes dominant in our culture, science has little future. In fact, Gary Zukav declares that 'we are approaching the end of science'.[15] This, he says, does not mean the end of the search for more comprehensive and useful physical theories. What it does mean is, as Professor G. F. Chew puts it, 'a completely new form of human intellectual endeavour, one that will not only lie outside physics but will not even be describable as "scientific"'.[16] This will be the result of entering into 'the higher dimensions of human experience'. This seems to imply that the current scientific laboratory will be replaced by a seance laboratory.

What may seem surprising is the fact that New Age writers appeal to modern science to vindicate their view of the nature of truth and reality. Marilyn Ferguson claims that 'the new science goes beyond cool, clinical observations to a realm of shimmering paradox, where our very reason seems endangered'.[17] The paradoxes can be accepted because

> On some level – call it heart, right brain, gut, collective unconscious – we recognize the rightness, even the simplicity of the principles involved. They fit with deeply buried knowledge within us. Science is only confirming

paradoxes and intuitions humankind has come across many times but stubbornly disregarded.[18]

Apparently the one place where these paradoxes and intuitions have not been disregarded is in the Eastern religious philosophies. Capra claims that

> . . . the basic elements of the Eastern world view are also those of the world view emerging from modern physics . . . Eastern thought and, more generally, mystical thought provide a consistent and relevant background to the theories of contemporary science.[19]

What is to be made of all this? I think that two things are going on here. First, there is an apologetic aimed at those who are sceptical of New Age thinking. Such people have a high regard for scientific truth, and so are being told that science (not the old science of Galileo, Bacon, Descartes and Newton, but the 'new science' of modern physics) supports the New Age view of reality. As is often the case with apologetics, it also provides support for the new or wavering New Age adherent. The appeal to modern physics seemed to have had this function for Shirley MacLaine at one point in her experience.[20] Secondly, there is an apologetic on behalf of science addressed to New Agers. This is Capra's stated aim in *The Tao of Physics*:

> This book aims at improving the image of science by showing that there is an essential harmony between the spirit of Eastern wisdom and Western science. It attempts to suggest that modern physics goes far beyond technology, that the way – or *Tao* – of physics can be a path with a heart, a way to spiritual knowledge and self-realization.[21]

Conclusion

New Agers regard traditional science as the archetypal left-brain activity. As such, it is castigated as a major cause of the problems of Western society. In theory its approach to understanding reality can be accepted as complementary to that of the right brain. In practice, however, the right-brain approaches are made primary because they allow experience of reality-as-it-is, not just of reality-as-it-appears in the physical world. But all is not lost for the scientist. It is claimed that there is a 'new science' which also puts us in touch with reality-as-it-is and that there is in fact a coming-together of Eastern mysticism and modern science.

3

THE NEW PHYSICS
AND NEW AGE THOUGHT

When claiming scientific support for their view of reality, New Agers often appeal to the 'new physics'. This is not a term which they invented, but it does have the advantage of paralleling the term 'New Age'. It is a term that is used to distinguish modern physics from what is now called 'classical physics', which is the physics based on the foundations laid by Galileo and Newton.

By the late nineteenth century classical physics seemed to provide an almost totally satisfactory amount of the material world. In 1900 the great physicist Lord Kelvin said that there were only two 'clouds' on the horizon of physics.[1] The first of these 'clouds' concerned the speed of light. In a series of experiments in the early 1880s, Michelson and Morley failed to find any difference in the apparent speed of light, whether it was measured in the direction of the Earth's motion or perpendicular to it. To appreciate the oddity of this, think about the motion of cars on the road. When driving on a road where everyone is travelling at 60–70 km per hour, a car coming up from behind to overtake us appears to be travelling much more slowly than one which is approaching us at the same speed. This is because the speeds at which the two cars are travelling *relative to us* are very different. The one overtaking us is approaching us at only a few kilometres per hour., whereas the other one is approaching us at a relative speed of over

120 km per hour. Now think of two cars approaching a crossroads. If, as one car crosses the junction at 60 km per hour, the other is approaching along the road to its right at the same speed, its apparent speed of approach will be 60 km per hour. This is what classical physics predicts with regard to light. Light travels at the finite, though great, speed of about 300,000 km per second. As it travels around the Sun, the Earth moves at about 30 km per second. Although this is much slower than the speed of light, the apparatus used by Michelson and Morley was sufficiently sensitive for them to have detected the difference between the apparent speed of light measured in the direction of the Earth's motion and that measured at right angles to it. They failed to detect any difference.

The second 'cloud' concerned the radiation of energy (in the form of heat and light) by a 'black body' – the term for the perfect type of radiator. Both heat and light can be thought of as waves of electro-magnetic energy. They differ only in the frequency at which the waves vibrate. Light is simply those waves which have a frequency which activates the nerves in our eyes so that we see them. At any given temperature a black body radiates waves at a whole range of frequencies. According to classical physics, the intensity of the radiation from a black body held at a fixed temperature should rise continuously with increasing frequency. However, this is not what happens. Experiments carried out by Lummer and Pringsheim between 1877 and 1900 showed that the intensity of the radiation rises to a maximum and then falls off sharply with increasing frequency. The position of the maximum shifts to a higher frequency as the temperature of the black body is raised.

These two 'clouds' burst in the early years of the twentieth century and blew apart the structure of classical physics. Out of them came, respectively, the theory of relativity and quantum theory, which form the heart of the 'new physics'.

The theory of relativity[2]

The answer to the problem of the speed of light was put forward by Albert Einstein in 1905. He proposed that the speed of light is a constant which has the same value no matter from what 'frame of reference' it is measured. In other words, he accepted as his starting-point that the speed of light will be the same in whatever direction it is measured with respect to the motion of the Earth. He also proposed the principle that nothing can travel faster than light.

These two seemingly simple propositions have some very profound and surprising implications. If the speed of light is the same whether measured when travelling at one tenth or at half the speed of light, the difference must lie in the measuring instruments. Put crudely, the ruler must change its length (the faster it moves the shorter it will become in the direction in which it is travelling) and the clock must run at different rates at the two speeds (it will run more slowly the faster it moves). The change in the clock leads to the 'twin paradox'. If one of a pair of twins leaves the Earth in a rocket and travels at close to the speed of light for some months, when he returns to Earth his twin will be several years older than he is, since time passes more slowly when measured on the faster-moving frame of reference. Since in everyday life we do not travel at anything more than a minute fraction of the speed of light, we are unaware of these phenomena. However, they have been proved true for sub-atomic particles moving at close to the speed of light.

Interesting as these predictions are, more important from our point of view are two other consequences of the theory. The first is the well-known equation:

$$E = mc^2$$

where E stands for 'energy', m for 'mass', and c for the speed of light. This states that matter and energy are equivalent and inter-convertible. It provided the key to nuclear power. Experiments in high-energy particle physics have verified this equation. It is now a well-established fact that sub-atomic particles can be converted into, or created from, energy. Also, one kind of particle can be converted into another with the absorption or emission of energy.

The second consequence is the unification of space and time. According to the theory of relativity, time can no longer be regarded as an independent entity separate from the three spatial dimensions of length, depth and height. Instead, we must think in terms of unified, four-dimensional, space-time. This puts a new slant on an old debate. Classical physicists debated whether or not there was such a thing as absolute space, *i.e.* a 'structure' existing separately from the material 'contents' of the universe. The debate now continues, but is about space-time.

Quantum theory[3]

Max Planck solved the black-body radiation problem. In 1899 he proposed that energy cannot be emitted or absorbed by a radiator in amounts of any quantity whatever, but only in 'packets' or 'quanta' of fixed amount. The amount depends on the frequency of the radiation carrying the energy and is expressed by the equation:

$$E = h\nu$$

in which ν stands for 'frequency' and h is an unchanging fundamental constant called 'Planck's constant'.

The idea that energy is 'quantized' has consequences as strange and far-reaching as the simple propositions behind relativity theory. One of the most famous is Heisenberg's Uncertainty Principle. Heisenberg showed that quantization puts limits on how accurately we can measure certain things. Suppose that we want to determine both the position (y) and the momentum (p = mass × velocity) of a material particle. Heisenberg showed that the uncertainty in the position (y) is related to the uncertainty in the momentum ($\triangle p$) by the equation:

$$\triangle y \times \triangle p \geqslant h/2$$

This means that the more precisely we know the position of the particle (the smaller $\triangle y$ is) the greater our uncertainty about its momentum (the larger $\triangle p$ becomes). Because of the size of Planck's constant (h), this problem becomes noticeable only at the small distances and masses that physicists meet at the atomic level. The best that they can do at this level is talk in terms of the probability that a particle is at position 'y', or has momentum 'p'.

What is the cause of this uncertainty? Einstein and Planck believed that it is a result of our ignorance, and that there are underlying factors as yet unknown to us which would remove our uncertainty if we knew them. Heisenberg believed that it is the result of a fundamental randomness inherent in the nature of reality.

By the end of the nineteenth century, light had come to be thought of as a wave of energy. This seemed the best way to explain its properties. However, in 1905 Einstein showed that the recently discovered 'photoelectric effect' could be explained only if light was regarded as a stream of energetic massless particles ('photons') whose energy is quantized according to Planck's equation. But this particle picture of light cannot explain other phenomena (such as diffraction) which are explained by the wave picture of light! To add to this puzzle, it was found that electrons (one of the constituents of the atom), which were initially regarded as negatively charged particles with a definite mass, sometimes behaved as if they were waves of energy with a wavelength (λ) related to their momentum (p) by the formula:

$$\lambda = h/p$$

On this basis Schrödinger developed a form of quantum theory called 'wave mechanics' which treats all sub-atomic phenomena in terms of the mathematics of waves.

The odd behaviour of light and electrons led physicists to accept the Principle of Complementarity. This is the recognition that some phenomena can be understood adequately only in terms of mutually exclusive but complementary pictures, like those of waves and particles. Because they are mutually exclusive, both pictures cannot be applied at one and the same time. What determines whether an electron behaves like a wave or a particle? One answer is that the experimental set-up we use to observe the electron determines this. In other words, *how* we look at it determines *what* we see.

A similar question can be asked about the position of an electron, given that quantum theory tells us that we can predict its position only in terms of probability. If there are finite probabilities of it being at positions y_1, y_2, y_3, y_4 and so on, what determines the fact that we actually see it at position y_2? Again, some suggest that the very act of observing it 'fixes' it at that position. It is argued from this that since it is humans who decide what to observe and how to observe it, human consciousness plays a part in determining the way the world is.

One way of resolving the wave–particle duality mathematically is a form of quantum theory called 'quantum field theory'. This treats 'particles' not as entities in themselves, but as the result of interactions between energy fields. Energy fields, like waves, spread out in space. Where two fields meet, they interact in a way that may have either wave-like or particle-like characteristics. This approach can be taken to imply that ultimate reality is a set of interacting energy fields.

The final aspect of quantum theory with which we shall deal is a paradox which was first pointed out by Einstein and two of his co-workers, Podolsky and Rosen. As a result, it is sometimes called 'the EPR paradox'. It is also called 'the Bell effect', after a physicist who carried out a mathematical analysis which provided the basis for an experimental test to demonstrate whether or not this paradox actually exists. Sometimes a sub-atomic event produces a pair of particles which fly off in different directions. Quantum theory predicts that from then on the characteristics of these two particles will be linked, however far apart they go. For example, sub-atomic particles have a characteristic called 'spin'. If, when the two particles are produced, one of them has a spin of $+1$ and the other has a spin of -1, throughout their lifetime their combined spin will always be zero. Now it is possible to change the spin of a particle. If the spin of one of the pair is changed from 1 to -1, quantum theory predicts that the spin of the other will instantaneously change from -1 to 1, even if it is millions of miles away. This is inexplicable by the normal law of causality. According to this, for one event to cause another information must travel between them. But the theory of relativity says that this cannot happen faster than the speed of light (information has to be carried by something – such as a light beam, or an electric current). So how is this instantaneous 'action at a distance' produced? No-one knows, but experiment shows that it is a reality. What happens to a particle in one part of the universe affects a particle in another, far-distant part without any physical cause-and-effect link.

The New Age claims

Faced with this 'new physics', Fritjof Capra claims that

> Although we are still lacking a complete quantum-relativistic theory of the sub-atomic world, several partial theories and models have been developed which describe some aspects of this world very successfully. A discussion of the most important of these models and theories will show that they all involve philosophical conceptions which are in striking agreement with those in Eastern mysticism.[4]

We will examine what Capra and others mean by considering a number of postulates which they claim are supported by both modern physics and Eastern mysticism.

1. *The material world we see is an illusion*

Ultimate reality, they claim, is an insubstantial flux of energy. Support for this is found in Einstein's equation:

$$E = mc^2$$

Both Capra and Zukav make much of the equivalence of matter and energy expressed in this equation. They take it to mean that matter is only transient and that energy is the ultimate reality. Zukav says:

> In the East, however, there never has been much philosophical or religious (only in the West are these two separate) confusion about matter and energy. The world of matter is a relative world, and an illusory one: illusory not in the sense that it does not exist, but illusory in the sense that we do not see it as it really is. The way it really is cannot be communicated verbally, but in the attempt to talk around it, eastern literature speaks repeatedly of dancing energy and transient, impermanent forms. This is

strikingly similar to the picture of physical reality emerging from high-energy particle physics.[5]

Capra puts it more succinctly:

> Like modern physicists, Buddhists see all objects as processes in a universal flux and deny the existence of any material substance.[6]

Further support is found in the success of quantum field theory as a way of dealing with the interactions of sub-atomic particles. Zukav claims that

> According to quantum field theory, fields alone are real. *They* are the substance of the universe and not 'matter'. Matter (particles) is simply the momentary manifestations of interacting fields which, intangible and insubstantial as they are, are the only real things in the universe.[7]

Capra appeals to a specific aspect of quantum field theory, namely the picture it gives of a vacuum. From the point of view of the theory a vacuum is a state in which the *average* energy is zero. Now, the Heisenberg Uncertainty Principle applies not only to the position of a particle and its momentum. It couples together other pairs of variables. One such pair is energy (E) and time (t), which are related by the equation:

$$\triangle E \times \triangle t \geqslant h/2$$

One implication of this is that one cannot say with absolute certainty at a specific point in time and space in a vacuum that the energy *is* zero. For fleeting periods, the energy at a particular point can be non-zero. The shorter the period (the smaller $\triangle t$) the greater the energy ($\triangle E$) can be. Because of the equivalence of matter and energy, the energy can, of course, appear in the form of sub-atomic particles. As a result, the vacuum of quantum field theory is not an absolute emptiness, but contains an unlimited number of sub-atomic particles coming into being for a few fleeting moments and then vanishing again. According to Capra, this means that quantum field theory provides

> . . . the closest parallel to the Void of Eastern mysticism in modern physics. Like the Eastern Void, the 'physical vacuum' – as it is called in field theory – is not a state of mere nothingness, but contains the potentiality for all forms of the particle world. These forms, in turn, are not independent physical entities but merely transient manifestations of the underlying Void.[8]

Capra dwells on this parallel at some length, comparing the patterns of creation and destruction of particles which physicists see in the tracks which such particles make in what are called 'cloud chambers' and 'bubble chambers' and the Hindu imagery of 'the dance of Shiva'. In Hindu belief, all life is part of a great rhythmic process of creation and destruction, of death and rebirth. Shiva is the Hindu god of creation and destruction. He maintains the ceaseless rhythm of the universe through his dance. In Hindu art he is depicted as the dancing god. Heinrich Zimmer describes the significance of these images of Shiva:

> His gestures wild and full of grace, precipitate the cosmic illusion; his flying arms and legs and the swaying of his torso produce – indeed, they are – the continuous creation-destruction of the universe, death exactly balancing birth, annihilation the end of every coming-forth.[9]

Capra asserts that

> The bubble-chamber photographs of interacting particles, which bear testimony to the continual rhythm of creation and destruction in the universe, are visual images of the dance of Shiva equalling those of the Indian artists in beauty and profound significance. The metaphor of the cosmic dance thus unifies ancient mythology, religious art, and modern physics.[10]

The claim that both relativity and quantum theory support the view that matter is an illusion is totally unconvincing. Einstein's equation says nothing more than that matter can be converted into energy and vice versa. It does not say, or even imply, that either matter or energy is more permanent or more real than the other. To say that matter is unreal because it can be converted into energy is like saying that ice is unreal because it can be turned into water.

Contrary to what Capra and Zukav say, quantum field theory simply shows that both energy-field and particle interpretations of sub-atomic reality are valid, depending on how that reality is 'interrogated' by us through the different forms of experiment we use.[11] Again, there is no necessary implication that one interpretation is more 'real' than another. Some people argue that, since quantum field theory gives the best and most workable description that we have of atomic and sub-atomic phenomena, and since it uses the mathematics of energy fields, it is reasonable to conclude that energy fields are the ultimate reality. However, caution is needed here. The success of quantum field theory may say more about the current state of our mathematical knowledge and sophistication than it does about the nature of ultimate reality. We should not forget that a hundred years ago a similar argument, based on classical physics, supported a different view of ultimate reality. Who knows what the outcome of such an argument might be a hundred years from now! It seems prudent to be cautious in drawing far-reaching metaphysical conclusions from physical theories.

The analogy between particle interactions and Shiva's dance makes the big assumption that there is a valid basis for drawing such an analogy between Hindu philosophical concepts and quantum theory. We will examine this assumption later. There is also another assumption which we need to examine later. This is that a description of the world of atomic and sub-atomic particles is indeed a description of 'ultimate reality'. Both of these assumptions run right through the thinking of Capra, Zukav, Talbot and other New Agers who write about physics, and so will be considered at the end of the next chapter.

2. *The universe must be seen as a unified, inter-connected whole*

The key piece of evidence for this second postulate is the EPR paradox, or Bell effect (described earlier on page 38). The essence of the paradox can be understood by considering the behaviour of snooker balls. When the cue ball strikes one of the other balls, the two balls move off in different directions. Their motion is not random, but obeys the laws of action and reaction discovered and codified by Newton. If the momentum of the cue ball before the collision is known, then measurement of the momentum of either ball after the collision enables the momentum of the other one to be calculated without it needing to be observed. The laws of action and reaction apply to atomic and sub-atomic particles. This ought to mean that if, after two particles have interacted, the momentum of particle 1 is measured, that of particle 2 can be deduced. Because of the Uncertainty Principle, this measurement will render the position of particle 1 uncertain but, since the momentum of particle 2 has not been measured directly, its position can be measured accurately. If this is done at the same time that the momentum of particle 1 is measured, both the position and momentum of particle 2 have been measured accurately, so circumventing the Uncertainty Principle. However, this argument makes two assumptions.

First, it assumes that a measurement made on a particle in one place cannot instantaneously affect a particle in another, relatively distant, place. This is called *the locality principle*. One reason for assuming this is that all normal physical effects are brought about by transfer of energy or information in some form and, according to the theory of relativity, this cannot happen at a speed faster than that of light. Though large, this is finite.

Second, it assumes that such things as 'position' and 'momentum' and 'particle' have an objective existence even when not observed. This is called *the reality principle*.

What Bell did was carry out the mathematical analysis which provided the basis for an experimental test of whether or not these two assumptions hold true for sub-atomic particles. The answer obtained by the experiment is that they do not. This means that one of the assumptions must be invalid. Most physicists prefer to dispense with the locality principle, at least with regard to quantum systems. This means that once two sub-atomic particles have interacted with one another, they are ever afterwards part of a single quantum system. As a result, if, for example, the momentum of one of them is changed, the momentum of the other will also change *instantaneously*. This will happen even if they are at opposite ends of the galaxy. The shocking thing about this is that it means that something other than normal 'cause and effect' is operating in quantum systems, though we cannot (yet) describe or define just what it is.

Zukav concludes that the Bell effect shows that

> . . . what happens here is intimately and immediately connected to what happens elsewhere in the universe, and so on, simply because the 'separate parts' of the universe are not separate parts.[12]

In other words, the universe is one single, interconnected wholeness and the 'separate parts' into which we divide it are unreal – as the Eastern mystics have told us all along.

There is a fundamental confusion in the way that Capra *et al.* appeal to the Bell effect. In fact, the Bell effect can be interpreted in two ways. The most popular interpretation is that there is instantaneous 'action at a distance' within a quantum system. The alternative interpretation is to abandon, not the locality principle, but the reality principle. This would mean accepting that there is no underlying physical reality corresponding to such abstract concepts as 'electron', 'position' or 'momentum'. The problem for Capra is that he wants to have it both ways. As we shall see, he denies the reality of electrons and their properties, but then also appeals to the Bell effect to prove the inter-relatedness of all things. To be consistent, he can appeal to the Bell effect to support only one or other of these points, not both.

A second line of argument arises from the fact that, according to the theory of relativity, time can no longer be regarded as an independent entity separate from the three spatial dimensions of length, depth and height. Instead, we have to think in terms of a unified, four-dimensional, space-time. The classical view is that events *happen* in three-dimensional space and *develop* with the passage of time, which flows in one direction. According to the theory of relativity, says Zukav,

> . . . it is preferable, and more useful, to think in terms of a *static*, non-moving picture of space–time . . . In this static picture, the space-time continuum, events do not develop, they just are. If we could view our reality in a four-

dimensional way, we would see that everything that now seems to unfold before us with the passing of time, already exists *in toto*, painted, as it were, on the fabric of space-time.[13]

Therefore, he argues, ultimate reality is a timeless unity, as Eastern mystics have always claimed.

The variability of the dimensions of space-time with the motion of the frame of reference, illustrated by the change in the length of rulers and the speed at which clocks run, leads Capra to conclude that there is no such thing as absolute space and time, but rather that space and time 'are nothing but names, forms of thought, words of common use', so that they are

. . . now reduced to the subjective role of the elements of the language a particular observer uses for his or her description of natural phenomena.[14]

Capra considers that there is a striking similarity between this relativistic notion of space-time and reality experienced by Eastern mystics when they attain

. . . non-ordinary states of consciousness in which they transcend the three-dimensional world of everyday life to experience a higher, multidimensional reality.[15]

In these states they are aware, he says, of the interpenetration of space and time.

The view that the theory of relativity requires a subjectivist interpretation of space and time is not universally accepted. Clifton and Regehr say that there are basically two metaphysical views of space-time.[16] There is *substantivalism*. This regards space-time as a kind of substance which exists separately, and has specifiable features, independent of the existence of the ordinary material objects which 'fill' it. In contrast, according to *relationism* the space-time structure is not real in itself, but only a systematic way of talking about spatial and temporal relations between material objects. The debate between those who hold these two positions continues to be a live one.

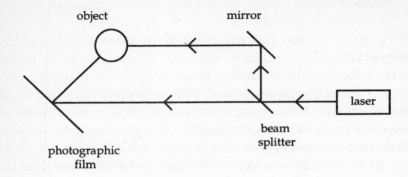

Diagram of the set-up used to produce a hologram. When the photographic film has been developed, shining a laser beam through the negative produces a three-dimensional image of the object.

Also, Capra's assertion that 'space and time are fully equivalent'[17] is particularly open to question. The fact is that we can move freely in space but not in time. Direction in time does not seem purely subjective or conventional. The 'before → after' direction in time appears much more objective than any direction in space.

An argument by analogy which is often appealed to in order to support the view that the universe is an inter-connected unity is that of the hologram. A hologram is produced by two beams of laser light, one striking a photographic film directly, the other being bounced off a three-dimensional object. When the developed film is illuminated by the same type of laser light, an image of the original object in three dimensions is produced. Moreover, only a small part of the film needs to be illuminated, showing that this small part contains the information of the whole. This, it is argued, supports the mystical view that the totality of reality is 'in' each part and that everything is intimately inter-connected. As Marilyn Ferguson puts it,

> . . . psychic phenomena are only by-products of the simultaneous-every-where matrix. Individual brains are bits of a greater hologram. They have access under certain circumstances to all the information in the total

46

cybernetic system . . . The brain is a hologram, interpreting a holographic universe.[18]

The idea of the holographic universe has been developed at length by Michael Talbot.[19]

The holographic paradigm is sometimes appealed to as if it provided *proof* of the inter-connectedness of all things. At best, however, it can provide no more than a model of how we might think about this, and especially about the mystics' experience of oneness with the universe. There are a number of weaknesses in this model.

1. As a hologram is cut into smaller and smaller fragments there is a loss of clarity of the image. Eventually no image can be produced at all. According to the mystics, however, the whole of reality is fully 'encoded' in each fragment, however small.

2. What corresponds to reality in the analogy is not really the photographic plate but the plate plus the necessary apparatus to reproduce the image, which has no parallel in the mystical view.

3. The hologram does not contain information about itself but about a separate objective reality. In order for a strict analogy to hold, the reality experienced by the mystic as 'in' each fragment of reality would have to be the copy of *another* real universe.

As in the case of appeal to Shiva's dance, we can see the limitations and dangers of argument by analogy.

3. Human consciousness plays a part in creating reality

We have seen that, as a result of quantum theory, physicists have had to accept that some phenomena can be understood adequately only in terms of mutually exclusive but complementary 'models' – the models of particles and waves. Because they are mutually exclusive, both pictures cannot be applied at one and the same time. If we ask, 'What determines whether an electron behaves like a wave or a particle?' one answer is that the experimental set-up we use to observe it determines this. In other words, *how* we look at it determines *what* we see. A similar situation applies to its position or momentum, *etc.*, given the Uncertainty Principle. If there are finite probabilities of it being in several different positions, or of its momentum, *etc.*, having various values, what determines the fact that we see it at one particular position or with a particular momentum? Again, some suggest that the very act of observing it 'fixes' its position or momentum, *etc*. It is argued from this that since it is humans who decide what to observe and how to observe it, human consciousness plays a part in determining the way the world is. As Capra puts it, 'The electron does not *have* properties independent of my mind.'[20] Humans are participators in the creation of reality. This leads Talbot to claim that

> For centuries the mystic has asserted that matter and consciousness are different aspects of the same *something*. For all those who have spent their lives trying to penetrate the secrets of matter, the new physics has a message, not a new one, but one that may well turn out to be the most important rediscovery humankind has ever made . . . the message of the new physics is that we are *participators* in a universe of increasing wonder.[21]

Shirley MacLaine picked up on this idea from her New Age friends. She says she discovered that

> Quantum physics was saying that what we perceive to be physical reality was actually our cognitive construction of it. Hence reality was only what each of us decided it was.[22]

Later she combines this with the idea of the cosmic dance:

> As the new physics and the ancient mystics now seemed to agree – when one observes the world and the beings within it, one sees that we are in fact only dancing with our own consciousness. Everything we feel, think and act upon is interrelated with everything everyone else feels, thinks, and acts upon. We are *all* participating in the dance.[23]

There are various difficulties in the position adopted by Capra and Talbot. One is that it is only one (and not the most widely held) of several possible interpretations of the implications of quantum theory. We will consider briefly the more common of these interpretations.[24]

One view is that the quantum theory describes not physical reality, but simply my knowledge of it. When a measurement 'fixes' the position of a particle, there has been no change in the state of the physical system. The change is in my state of knowledge. The question of where that knowledge comes from is ignored. Although this may seem a simple solution to the problem, it is not one that is to be adopted lightly. It reduces physics to a branch of psychology. It abandons the idea of knowledge originating outside of ourselves in a physical world that stands over against us, and about which we can discover real knowledge. Instead we are left with mental images only, the ground of which is left obscure.

Secondly, there is the view that it is human consciousness which determines the state of quantum systems. These systems are in an undetermined state until the intervention of a conscious observer. This view has been expressed in a number of variant forms. One weakness they all have is that none of them explains how consciousness and quantum systems interact and why the result should be a 'fixing' of the state of the system. Also, they face the common-sense objection that they imply that, in those parts of the universe where there are no conscious observers, everything is still undetermined. To bring it closer to home, they also imply that photographs taken of particle events in a cloud chamber and stored away in a drawer, uninspected, acquire an image only when someone opens the drawer and looks at them. Another problem with this interpretation of quantum theory is that it is implicitly solipsistic. The only world I can really know about is the one I experience or create. One of the characteristics of orthodox modern science is that experimental results are acceptable only if they can be repeated by any experimenter anywhere who follows the set experimental procedure. If the consciousness of the observer is all-important, this would have to include the consciousness of the original experimenter!

In any case, it is not clear that the appeal that Capra *et al.* make to this view is legitimate. Thus Capra says:

> The human observer constitutes the final link in the chain of observational processes, and the properties of any atomic object can only be understood in terms of the object's interraction with the observer. This means that the

classical ideal of an objective description of nature is no longer valid. The Cartesian partition between the I and the world, between the observer and the observed, cannot be made when dealing with atomic matter.[25]

Here the second and third sentences do not follow from the first. In fact, the interpretation of quantum theory that Capra is espousing rests on the *distinction* between observer and observed and on the *difference* between consciousness and the 'matter' of the observed quantum world which results in the interaction between the two having the effect it is claimed to have. Interestingly, Capra recognizes this, and implicitly contradicts his earlier assertion, when he admits that

> The mystics are not satisfied with a situation analogous to atomic physics, where the observer and observed cannot be separated, but can still be distinguished. They go much further, and in deep meditation they arrive at a point where the distinction between observer and observed breaks down completely, where subject and object fuse into a unified undifferentiated whole.[26]

A third view of quantum theory is the 'many worlds interpretation' proposed by Hugh Everett III. He suggests that in every situation in which there is a choice of experimental outcome because of quantum uncertainty, each possibility is in fact realized. The world splits up into many worlds, in each of which one of the possible results of the measurement actually occurs. These worlds exist alongside one another but there can be no communication between them. These worlds, of course, go on splitting endlessly.

The bizarre nature of this view gets it a good press in popular scientific publications. Some of Everett's fellow cosmologists espouse it as a way of getting around some of their problems. Most scientists, however, object to it, because it goes against the fundamental principle of 'Occam's Razor', that one should not multiply hypotheses (or entities) unnecessarily in order to explain a phenomenon. An infinite number of universes seems an unnecesssarily high price to pay to explain one aspect of quantum theory!

The most widely held view of quantum theory is what is called 'the

Copenhagen Interpretation', because it was worked out by Neils Bohr and his collaborators in Copenhagen. This proposes that, when we observe a quantum system, things get 'fixed' along the chain of correlated consequences once the objects with which we deal have become 'large'. To put it in other words, it is the interaction of classical measuring instruments with quantum systems which results in the 'fixing'. A conscious observer need not be involved at all. All that an observer has to do is note the output of the instrument. There are at least two obvious problems with this interpretation. First, it does not define how big 'large' has to be to give the effect of 'fixing' the state of the quantum system. Secondly, it does not explain how the intervention of the 'large' classical instrument chooses one chain of consequences rather than another on a particular occasion.

It is a strange situation. In laboratories all over the world, physicists are continually making measurements on quantum systems. Quantum theory triumphantly predicts, in terms of probabilities, what their outcomes will be. The theory is a great success. Yet we do not understand what is going on! Probably the best moral to draw from this is the one drawn by Clifton and Regehr:

> It is treading on thin ice to attach a particular religious philosophy to the viability of often ephemeral physical theories, especially when one is insensitive to the true contentiousness and depth of the interpretive issues involved.[27]

Capra and other New Agers seem to suffer from the insensitivity spoken of here. They never discuss, or even admit the existence of, the variety of interpretations that there are of quantum theory.

There is also, once again, the question whether the kind of interaction between consciousness and matter posited on the basis of quantum theory is really the same kind of thing that the Eastern mystics talk about. We will return to this issue in chapter 4 (see pages 55–58).

4. To understand reality we have to abandon classical logic

We have to replace the either/or of classical logic by both/and. As a result reality can be known only by experience.

Logic is the discipline which attempts to distinguish bad reasoning from good reasoning.[28] It attempts to formulate rules which can tell us whether the reasons that have been given for a particular conclusion are good ones or not. These rules form a logical system. The essential requirement of any logical system is that it should be self-consistent. The rules or 'laws' of a logical system are so framed that, if they are applied properly, it will not be possible to use them to prove statements which are mutually contradictory within the framework of the system. The logic which we use in everyday discussions and debate, so-called 'classical logic', makes use of rules which have been discussed and formulated since at least the time of Aristotle.

In 1936 von Neumann and Birkhoff laid the foundations for 'quantum logic'.[29] The most important difference between the rules of classical logic and quantum logic involves the law of distributivity. This law says that 'A, and B or C' means the same as 'A and B, or A and C'. For example, 'John is at home and is asleep or awake' means the same as 'John is at home and is asleep, or John is at home and is awake'. The law of distributivity is a foundation of classical logic, but it does not apply to quantum logic. This is why quantum mechanics can produce the wave–particle duality.

David Finkelstein appeals to quantum logic to argue that in the realm of experience nothing is *either* this *or* that but that there is always at least one more alternative. With regard to quantum theory he says:

> There are no waves in the game. The equation that the game obeys is a wave equation, but there are no waves running around . . . There are no particles running around either. What's running around are quanta, the third alternative.[30]

Quantum logic, he argues, is more real than classical logic because it is not based on a set of theoretical rules, the way we choose to think about things, but on the way we experience things. For example, he says:

> If you want to envision a quantum as a dot then you are trapped. You are modelling it with classical logic. The whole point is that there *is no* classical representation for it. We have to learn to live with the experience.

Question: How do you communicate the experience?

Answer: You don't. But by telling how you make quanta and how you measure them, you enable others to have it.[31]

Finkelstein seems to be making three claims.

1. Classical logic is a theoretical system of rules that has had the effect of constraining human thought and language in an artificial way.

2. Quantum logic, by contrast, arises from experience: the experience of the ultimate reality, the energy fields of quantum physics.

3. Subjective experience is the ultimate form of knowledge and it is strictly incommunicable by any kind of logical, and so rational, communication.

The contrast made here between classical and quantum logic is largely invalid. Classical logic is not a purely theoretical system invented by scholars living in ivory towers who were unconcerned about any correspondence between their logical arguments and ordinary people's experience of life. The laws of classical logic are derived from experience of what kinds of reasoning make 'good sense' of our experience of the world. They have been a great success in this regard. The problem which now faces us is that this logic which makes good sense of the macro-world seems to fail when applied to the micro-world of atoms and sub-atomic particles. This raises the question of the relative status of classical logic and quantum logic.

The question is a difficult one. P. Gibbins says that there are two opinions about it.[32] In the view of a small minority, quantum logic is supposed to be the real logic of the macro-world as well as the micro-world. This faces the problem of the tremendous success of classical logic in the macro-world, which seems to count against the validity of quantum logic at that level. The majority view is that there are two logics, each appropriate to its own domain, the micro-world and the macro-world. The problem then is how to account for the logical 'cut' between the two worlds. Unlike the case of mechanics, there is no smooth transition from one world to another in the limit of large quantum numbers. This brings us to an interesting consideration. Which world is the 'real' world, the quantum world or the world of everyday experience? We will return to this question later (see pages 61–63).

4

PHYSICS AND EASTERN MYSTICISM

On several occasions we have questioned the validity of the claims that New Agers have made about the similarity between, or even the identity of, the concepts of Eastern mysticism and those of modern physics. It is now time to look at this issue more closely. Here I must confess my lack of expertise and rely heavily on what those who are experts in Eastern philosophies have to say.

Richard Jones, among others, has criticized the way in which Capra *et al.* appeal to Eastern mysticism. He shows how they draw selectively on those concepts which suit their purpose but ignore others, equally important to a proper understanding of Eastern mysticism, which do not fit the scheme they want to portray. For example, he points out that the most important characteristic of the 'Eastern world-view' for Capra is the awareness of the unity and inter-connectedness of all things and events, and the experience of phenomena as manifestations of a basic oneness. This is not true of at least one major Eastern tradition, Advaita. Jones comments, 'Any account of Eastern thought that ignores this must remain a truncated one.'[1]

Scientists such as Capra are also open to the criticism that they too readily find modern concepts in Eastern mysticism. Jones asserts:

There is no conception in classical India of space and time combined or of

55

either time or space as an especially fundamental reality . . . Mystics have nothing comparable to a conception of unified space-time.[2]

One would never guess this, when reading Capra and Zukav! A specific criticism that Jones makes of Capra is that

His reasoning is often of this sort: because science and mysticism each have difficulty with language, they are talking about the same thing.[3]

Of Zukav's comparisons between Eastern thought and ideas in modern physics, Jones says that they are 'disconcerting at best', and goes on to criticize three examples in detail.[4] The following quotations sum up the essence of his criticisms:

There is nothing comparable in Buddhism to the virtual particle inter-actions: virtual particles apparently arise randomly, not in the orderly process as with Buddhist dependence . . . Nor is the distinction between virtual and 'real' particles similar to the distinction in Buddhism (and many other metaphysical systems) between reality as it actually is and as it usually seems to be.

Zukav, like many others, also sees paradoxes in physics as Zen *koans* . . . But, most important, *koans* represent a nonassertive approach to reality (i.e. no assertions about reality are involved), while science always remains assertive. Working through paradoxes . . . may also be part of both science and mysticism, but their scope is different: 'enlightenment' in physics is only to a new theory of limited scope, not to a new vision of all aspects of reality.

To assert further that in the East there never was much confusion about matter and energy . . . is also wrong: 'energy' in any recognizable scientific sense and the relation of it to matter are not topics dealt with in any classical Asian religious tradition.

A pertinent point to consider is whether the mystic and the physicist agree about 'how it really is'. Jones denies that this is the case. Among other things, he points out that mystics do not see energy fields but experience

> . . . a blending of objects in the sense that boundaries are less noticed in the light of impermanence and the common experienced being-ness.[5]

Moreover, this being-ness is something that is felt as a change in experience, not an abstract concept neutral to experience which can be expressed mathematically. He concludes:

> Mysticism focuses upon the identity of *being* while science focuses upon *structures*. Space-time has the structure necessary to explain why one specific cosmological state of affairs is the case; the depth-mystical identity is structureless and its relation to any structured unity of parts remains a mystery.

Finally, there is the question whether the kind of interaction between consciousness and matter posited on the basis of quantum theory is really the same kind of thing that the Eastern mystics talk about. Again, Jones concludes that it is not.

> There are some errors committed by those writing on matter-consciousness holism. First, nature-mysticisms such as Buddhism do not discuss the interaction of perceiver and object in perception: the perceiver, each act of perception, and the object of perception are analyzed without asserting that consciousness affects the object or vice versa. The most usual Indian view is that the mind modifies itself to the shape of any object in an act of perception – no interaction is involved. Obviously, 'participation' is an inappropriate description in this regard. The mystical interest is in whether what is seen is real or not – *knowledge*, not control or effects, is what is crucial.[6]

Jones finds that none of the ideas based on quantum theory of how consciousness affects what is observed can be compared with the mystical concept of creation by awareness. He also points out that causing a world (which is the mystical view) is different from causing only a limited number of events within a world (which, strictly, is what is proposed in relation to observing quantum events).

To sum up these criticisms: Capra *et al.* are taking disputed metaphysical interpretations of the implications of the theory of relativity and quantum theory and equating them with a selective, and therefore questionable, reconstruction of the Eastern mystical world-view. Moreover, they often seem to misunderstand the Eastern views and, perhaps as a result, assert invalid comparisons and identities between Eastern concepts and those used in modern physics.

Science and reductionism

As a Christian, I find myself in agreement with many of the negative things that New Agers say about science. What they are criticizing, however, is not really science or the scientific method, but what can be called 'scientism'. By this I mean a metaphysical construct which takes as one of its basic assumptions the belief that the scientific method is the only valid route to truth and that it therefore potentially provides us with a comprehensive view of reality. Such a construct is, of course, not a necessary consequence of embracing the scientific method, and one can do perfectly good science without accepting it.

The rejection of reductionism as a metaphysical stance, for example, does not mean that we have to reject the reductionist methodology of the physical sciences and the results it has obtained. What we do have to do is recognize that use of this methodology limits what can be studied and the kind of answers that can be obtained. Other approaches to truth-seeking are needed if we are to understand reality in its fullness. There is evidence from within science of the limitations of a reductionist methodology. Arthur Peacocke points out that there are scientific theories and concepts which are essential for understanding systems at a particular level of complexity, but which have no place at the lower level that results when the system is taken apart, and which cannot be explained by the theories that apply at the lower level.[7] This, he argues, means that as systems increase in complexity, truly novel phenomena appear which cannot be explained in a reductionist way.

The whole *is* more than the sum of the parts. Nevertheless, it is still valid, and valuable, to study the parts, as long as it is remembered that this gives an incomplete picture of the whole.

Christians cannot accept a metaphysical-reductionist view of human beings, *i.e.* that the human person can be specified totally and solely in terms of the physics and chemistry of matter. There is a human spirit, made in the image of its Creator, which, though expressed through the material body, is not to be simply identified with it. This, however, does not mean acceptance of a sharp Cartesian dualism. This 'spirit' need not to be thought of as another 'bit' which could be discovered along with the other bits by a reductionist methodology. It is more like the meaning of this paragraph. The meaning is not to be identified with the letters which carry it. No amount of study of the individual letters, or even words, in isolation will reveal the existence of the meaning. It can be found only when the paragraph is taken as a whole. Of course the meaning will disappear if the letters are erased. However, it will not cease to exist, because it still exists in my mind. I can express it again, perhaps in different letters (Greek or Hebrew). This is a helpful analogy for thinking about the Christian doctrine of bodily resurrection. It also seems to be in accord with the biblical presentation of the human person. Wheeler Robinson sums up the view of Old Testament scholars when he says, 'The Hebrew idea of personality is that of an animated body, not (like the Greek) that of an incarnated soul.'[8] The use of the more extensive Greek vocabulary for parts or aspects of the person in the New Testament might give the impression of a shift to a less unitary view, but a study of the use of them shows that this is not so. This 'animated body' view of the human person lies behind the concept of resurrection of the body (as against existence as a disembodied soul) as the destiny of humans. As well as avoiding a sharp dualism, this view avoids the monism of New Age thought which declares that matter is an illusion and identifies consciousness with the energy field that is supposed to be ultimate reality.

Reductionist philosophies have great difficulty in preserving any concept of human dignity because their logical conclusion is that we are nothing but robots programmed by the impersonal laws of physics. It seems that some New Agers regard the suggestion that the consciousness of the observer affects the matter which is observed (at least at the atomic level) as a way out of the mechanistic strait-jacket. However, it is an illusory one. By identifying consciousness with the quantum energy field, these New Agers make it something which is determined solely by the laws of physics. If appeal is made to the probabilistic nature of quantum events, it must be pointed out that this does not provide a basis for belief in free, responsible behaviour. Rather, it suggests random, capricious behaviour. For Christians, the basis for human dignity is the belief that each individual bears the image of God. It is this 'image-bearing' nature of humans which gives Christians (and gave the early modern scientists)[9] confidence in human rationality and objective truth, as will be argued below (see pages 61–63).

New Agers claim that they are opposed to being reductionist. However, when they assert that the world of quantum field theory is the real world, on the basis of which we have to interpret all our experiences, they are being just that. They are assuming that ultimate reality is to be found by reducing everything to the level of sub-atomic particles. At this level, they claim, we see that everything is bound up in an inter-related oneness. Therefore, they conclude, the separateness and individuality which we see at the macro-level of everyday experience are an illusion. Why should we not turn the tables and take our experience of the macro-world as the touchstone of reality? Even better, why not accept that at different levels of complexity novel realities arise, such as individual human consciousness, which are not 'illusions'?

Physics and trinitarianism

The evidence of the inter-related oneness of all things (at least at the sub-atomic level, provided by the testing of the Bell effect) does not cause me, as a Christian, any problems. If the universe is the creation of the one and only Creator, who constantly keeps it in being, one might expect there to be a fundamental coherence and unity about it if, as Christians believe, that Creator is a being whose actions are character-ized by rationality and reliability. Moreover, the Christian concept of

God is trinitarian; the one God is a harmonious inter-relationship of persons. It is not surprising if the creation reflects something of this as, like all great works of art, it reflects something of its Creator's nature.

The assertion that, because of this inter-connectedness of all things, the separate parts into which we, with our analytical thinking, divide the universe are unreal is, however, problematic. It does not seem to follow from the physics. Capra *et al*. seem to postulate this solely on the basis of their monistic metaphysics. On the basis of a trinitarian metaphysic, one can postulate the view that it is possible to have a harmonious unity within which there is no loss of diversity and individual identity.

This brings us back to the question raised at the end of the discussion of classical and quantum logic. Which world is the 'real' world – the micro-world or the macro-world; the world of undifferentiated quantized energy fields, equated with a universal consciousness, or the world of differentiated, individual, personal consciousness?

In the preface to *The Tao of Physics*, Capra tells us why he takes the option he does. The reason has nothing to do with science. It is 'a beautiful experience' he had one summer afternoon, sitting by the ocean watching the sunlight reflecting off the waves, when he felt the atoms of his body participating in the 'cosmic dance of energy'. On this basis he makes a leap from physics to metaphysics, identifying the *physical* energy fields of quantum theory with the *psychic* or *spiritual* energy about which mystics speak. He has every right to do this, but he does not really seem to be aware that he is making a tremendous assumption here. He does not try to justify it except by pointing out the apparent parallels between statements of mystics and of modern physicists which Richard Jones criticizes.

A Christian has as much right as Capra to choose to understand science within his or her own metaphysical framework. In this case it is belief in an infinite, self-existent, personal God who created an ordered universe and sustains it in being. Hence there is an objective reality which exists independently of human minds. Humans were created in the image of God. Therefore our minds correspond to God's and can understand the universe and the order which characterizes it. Of course, our understanding of reality will always be limited (because of our finiteness) and distorted (being coloured by our beliefs and opinions). That, however, does not make the search for objective knowledge pointless. It does mean that we have to accept that, at any one time, our knowledge is only a provisional approximation to the reality we are studying. Since all humans are rational beings sharing God's image and experiencing the same created, objective world, it seems reasonable to expect that experience to be communicable in a rational way, even if an exhaustive account of the experience cannot be given like this.[10] Moreover, the trinitarian view of God makes the ultimate reality a unified, yet differentiated, personal consciousness. Therefore the Christian will not be prepared to reject the differences manifest in the macro-world as illusory. Nor, as we have seen above, is there any need to deny the reality of the unity displayed at the sub-atomic level.

But what are we to make of the mystical experience of oneness – which, by the way, is not limited to Eastern religions but is also found in Islam, Judaism and Christianity? I can only make some tentative suggestions. The mystic may be experiencing the harmony and unity of God's creation. This can rightly lead to a sense of awe and wonder which stimulates worship of God. To go on seeking this experience of oneness *for itself*, however, is to take the road to idolatry, to put the creation in the place due to the Creator. Alternatively, the mystic may have a genuine experience of God, who is one. However, I question whether this is so when the experience is said to lead to a loss of personal identity. The biblical picture of God is of trinity – diversity in unity – not undifferentiated oneness. One biblical picture of our relationship with God is that of human lovers, husband and wife. In such a relationship there is a unity which comes from each partner's giving himself or herself to the other. But there is also an individuality which results from each accepting and affirming the other's worth. Indeed, as beings made in the image of God, we truly find ourselves only in finding a personal relationship of love and obedience towards God. In this we are affirmed in our individuality because we discover how much we are worth to God. His valuation of us has been declared by the sacrifice at Calvary.

There are two significant differences between appeal to the theistic

Christian metaphysical framework with regard to science and appeal to the monistic metaphysics of the New Age. The first is that the Christian framework is open to at least a degree of public verification, since at the heart of Christianity lie the historical events associated with Jesus of Nazareth as recorded in the Christian Gospels. The New Age framework rests on an incommunicable subjective experience. The second difference is that modern science grew up in, and was to a considerable degree based on, the Christian framework. As we have seen, the New Age framework, as Zukav recognizes,[11] will ultimately bring about the end of science.

5

PIERRE TEILHARD DE CHARDIN AND NEW AGE THOUGHT

In her book *The Aquarian Conspiracy*, Marilyn Ferguson reports the result of a survey of the views of 'two hundred and ten persons engaged in social transformation in many different areas'.[1] The person most often named as a profound influence on the 185 who responded was Pierre Teilhard de Chardin. When asked to designate which of a list of ideas had been important in their own thinking, 35% chose Teilhard's concept of evolving consciousness. One reason why Ferguson chose the word 'conspiracy' for the title of her book was Teilhard's call for a 'conspiracy of love'.[2] She makes it clear that she means 'conspiracy' in its literal sense of 'breathing together' and not in any political sense (a fact that many Christian have failed to realize). In her view,

> Teilhard prophesied the phenomenon central to this book: a conspiracy of men and women whose new perspective would trigger a critical contagion of change.[3]

Fritjof Capra also considers Teilhard as an important and revolutionary figure. He says:

Teilhard de Chardin has often been ignored, disdained, or attacked by scientists unable to look beyond the reductionist Cartesian framework of their disciplines. However, with the new systems approach to the study of living organisms, his ideas will appear in a new light and are likely to contribute significantly to general recognition of the harmony between the views of scientists and mystics.[4]

What attracts New Age thinkers to Teilhard is his interpretation of the biological theory of evolution in terms of the evolution of consciousness, and so we need to turn to an examination of this interpretation. Before that, however, a brief sketch of Teilhard's life will provide a helpful background.

Pierre Teilhard de Chardin

Teilhard was born on 1 May 1881 in the family home, Sarcenat, near Clermont in the Auvergne district of central France. He was the fourth of eleven children in a devout Roman Catholic family. His father was a scholarly country gentleman. Teilhard's interest in biology was stimulated by his father, who opened his eyes to his surroundings. He once wrote:

> Auvergne moulded me . . . Auvergne served me both as museum of natural history and as wild-life preserve . . . to Auvergne I owe my delight in nature.[5]

His mother also had an important influence on him. On hearing of her death, when he was in his fifties, he said, 'To this dear and sainted mother I owe the best part of my soul.'[6]

At the age of eleven he went to a Jesuit college, where he developed a particular interest in geology and mineralogy. When he was eighteen he joined the Society of Jesus as a novice. After only two years of study the Society was expelled from France and his seminary moved to Jersey. This was the start of his association with Britain. He also developed a great interest in the fossil-bearing rocks which abound in Jersey.

In 1905 he went to Cairo for three years to teach chemistry and physics in a Jesuit school. Here he wrote and had published his first scholarly papers, on the Eocene strata in Egypt. He then returned to Britain, to a Jesuit House in Hastings, for a customary four years' study of theology. A year after being ordained priest in 1911, he returned to France to undertake serious work in geology and palaeontology. During a return visit to Hastings in 1913 he visited the site where the Piltdown skull had been unearthed, in the company of its discoverer Dr Dawson. He picked up a canine tooth which, like the skull, was unmasked forty years later as a forgery. When the fraud was discovered he wrote to Dr Oakley of the British Museum, saying:

> I congratulate you most sincerely on your solution of the Piltdown problem. Anatomically speaking, 'Eoanthropus' was a kind of monster. And, from a palaeontological point of view it was equally shocking that a 'dawn-man' should occur in England. Therefore I am fundamentally pleased by your conclusions, in spite of the fact that, sentimentally speaking, it spoilt one of my brightest and earliest palaeontological memories.[7]

During the First World War he served as a stretcher-bearer and was decorated three times for his bravery under fire. During this period he developed a feeling of oneness with the whole of humankind, and the idea of the cosmic Christ. These concepts were to form an essential part of his evolutionary thought.[8]

After the war he resumed his scientific career, and in 1920 became Professor of Geology at the Catholic Institute of Paris. In 1923 he went to China on a palaeontological mission. His experience of the desert remoteness of Mongolia led him to see that everything in the world could be described in terms of one single activity. As he put it in a letter to a friend:

> Now in the vast solitudes of Mongolia (which from the human point of view are a static and dead region), I see the same thing as I saw long ago at the 'front' (which from the human point of view was the most alive thing that existed): one single operation is in process of happening in the world,

and it alone can justify our action: the emergence of some spiritual reality, through and across the efforts of life.[9]

This view gained expression in his *Mass on the World*, in which he, as God's priest, offered up to God 'on the altar of the entire earth, the travail and the suffering of the world'.[10]

When he returned to Paris in 1924, his ideas about original sin and its relation to evolution were considered unorthodox by his superiors and he was forbidden to continue teaching. His ideas, however, were spread by students and others who discussed them with him and read private copies of his essays. Eventually, in 1926, he returned to China, where he lived and worked, with only occasional visits to Europe, for some twenty years. In 1938 he was appointed Director of the Laboratory of Advanced Studies in Geology and Palaeontology in Paris, but his return to France was prevented by the outbreak of the Second World War. Soon after his return to China he completed what some regard as his most profound book, *Le Milieu divin*. It is an essay on the inner life in which he attempted to

> . . . recapitulate the eternal lesson of the Church in the words of a man who, because he believes himself to feel deeply in tune with his own times, has sought to teach how to see God everywhere, to see him in all that is most hidden, most solid, and most ultimate in the world.[11]

His superiors would not allow the book to be published at the time.

Teilhard's years in China were very productive in terms of palaeontological work and publications. His best-known contribution was his association with the finding and description of *Sinanthropus* (Peking Man), an important example of one form of early hominid. When the Japanese occupation of China restricted his scientific work he spent the time revising the manuscript of the book which summarizes much of his thought, *The Phenomenon of Man*.

When he returned to France in 1946 he was still refused permission to publish his books, and his freedom to teach was restricted. Moreover, his Jesuit superiors would not let him accept a prestigious Chair in the Collège de France. Despite these disappointments Teilhard refused to consider leaving the Society, which he believed God had called him to join. In the early post-war years he travelled quite widely and made many contacts with leading scientists. One of these was Sir Julian Huxley, with whom he formed a deep friendship despite their widely differing philosophies of life. In 1951 his superiors insisted that he leave Paris. For the remaining four years of his life he lived in New York, working at the Wenner-Gren Foundation.

At the time of his death in 1955 Teilhard's influence was limited to his circle of work colleagues, friends and acquaintances. He had published over 150 scientific papers, but his philosophical-theological writings had been suppressed by his Jesuit superiors. The manuscripts of his writings were left to a friend, and so began to be published after his death, starting with *The Phenomenon of Man* (the French edition in 1955, and the English, with an Introduction by Sir Julian Huxley, in 1959). Although in 1962 the Holy Office issued a *Monitum* decree, warning bishops and heads of Catholic seminaries of dangers in Teilhard's writings, his posthumous works were not proscribed.

In the 1960s and 1970s 'Teilhardism' was quite a flourishing movement. Some even spoke of Teilhard as another Aquinas, bringing the benefits of pagan learning within the Christian fold.[12] In 1970 the English theologian Anthony Hanson could say:

> Teilhard's influence in this country shows no sign of decreasing. Those who offer to lecture on his work up and down the country report a sustained interest in him among a very wide section of the public, by no means confined to what would normally be called the religious public.[13]

Since the end of the seventies, however, Teilhardism does seem to have waned in the English-speaking world – except in a transmuted form among New Age thinkers.

The essentials of Teilhard's thought

Any attempt to give a brief summary of Teilhard's thought is bound to be unsatisfactory. His thought was complex and his ideas scattered throughout numerous essays and letters written over many years. His tendency to invent and use new words does not make it easy for the beginner to grasp his ideas readily. For our purposes, however, it is enough to concentrate on his major work, *The Phenomenon of Man*. It is not a complete summary of his thought, but it does contain the essence of it. Moreover, he claims that it is a scientific treatise, and it is this claim that allows New Age thinkers to appeal to Teilhard for scientific support for their ideas. His ideas will be outlined before attempting a critique of them in the next chapter.[14]

The foundation of Teilhard's thinking was the idea of biological evolution. Towers claims that, although he was not the first person to formulate some of the problems posed by evolution,

> He was the first to grasp the immensity of the change in thinking to which this discovery must give rise, and he was the first to enunciate, both in general outline and at times in great detail, what the Christian message really means in the light of this shattering new insight into the nature of things.[15]

As a result of his evolutionary outlook, a theme that runs through Teilhard's writings is *genesis* or becoming. He did not limit this to the biological world, but extrapolated it to the whole universe, to *cosmogenesis*. For Teilhard genesis is not simply a process, it is a *progress*, an *orthogenesis*, a development in a straight line towards a set goal. It was an essential part of his belief that progress is real and that it can, in a sense, be controlled by humans. Thus he could say:

> If progress is a myth, that is to say, if faced by the work involved we can say: 'What's the good of it all?' our efforts will flag. With that the whole of evolution will come to a halt – because we are evolution.[16]

There is a debate about exactly what he meant by 'progress'. R. B. Smith takes the key to be Teilhard's statement that the direction of human evolution is towards '*increased power for increased action*'.[17] He then concludes that for Teilhard it does not mean

. . . a necessary claim that we are better than our fathers, but a recognition that our opportunities are greater, and therefore our responsibilities more frightening: a thesis few would care to deny. In this sense progress is fundamental to the theme of *The Phenomenon*.[18]

This, however, presents too neutral a view of progress in *The Phenomenon of Man*. For Teilhard power for action is not an end in itself, but can be used for either good or evil. While he does contemplate the possibility that we could end up as a divided humanity on a materially exhausted planet, the whole thrust of the book is optimistic, tending to the view that the outcome will be much more positive:

> Disease and hunger will be conquered by science . . . hatred and internecine struggles will have disappeared . . . some sort of unanimity will reign . . . The final convergence will take place *in peace*.[19]

This gives an understandable idea of progress in human society, but in what sense can progress be seen in the non-human domain?

A key concept for Teilhard is what he called the *Law of Complexity-Consciousness*. This law states two things.[20]

1. Throughout time there has been a tendency in evolution for matter to become more complex in its organization.

2. With increase in material complexity there is a corresponding rise in the consciousness of the matter.

But in what sense can consciousness exist in, say, a stone or a plant? Teilhard wanted a coherent explanation of the universe which would take everything into account. A materialist explanation is inadequate because it recognizes only the material (or external) aspect, the 'without' of objects and persons. On the other hand, traditional spiritual interpretations tend to concentrate solely on the spiritual (or inner) aspects, the 'within' of people or events. A coherent explanation must put the two aspects together. People clearly have both a 'without' and a 'within'. These are not two separate entities (body and soul), but two different aspects of our existence as persons. Working back from humans, Teilhard argues that all matter must be viewed as having a without and a within, and so as possessing a form of consciousness. Of course the within varies with respect to the without. The within is most developed in humans, the most complex entity in the universe.[21]

In Teilhard's view, the increasing complexity of matter in cosmogenesis has come about not by a purely random process, but because matter has an internal propensity to unite. This tendency he called *radial energy*, to distinguish it from the long-recognized form of energy which behaves in accordance with the laws of thermodynamics, which he called *tangential energy*. This leads him to treat all forms of energy as of one kind – psychic in nature:

> We shall assume that, essentially, all energy is psychic in nature; but add that in each particular element this fundamental energy is divided into two distinct components: a *tangential energy* which links the element with all others of the same order (that is to say, of the same complexity and the same centricity) as itself in the universe; and a *radial energy* which draws it towards ever greater complexity and centricity – in other words forwards.[22]

In a footnote to the quote about progress cited earlier, Teilhard says, 'All conscious energy is, like love (and because it is love), founded on hope.'[23] Later on he speaks of love as the expression at the human level of radial energy, the internal propensity to unite.[24]

For Teilhard the process of evolution is not a smooth one. There are a number of critical points in it. He compares these to physical changes of state, such as the melting of a solid or the boiling of a liquid, which occur as temperature is increased smoothly. They are 'jumps of all sorts *in the course* of development'.[25] The advent of life is one such 'critical singular point, an unparalleled moment on the curve of telluric evolution, a point of *germination*'.[26] What he seems to be doing here is stressing the uniqueness and never-to-be-repeated character of the event, rather than implying that there is no 'natural' explanation for it.

The advent of human consciousness was a major critical point in evolution. But what characterizes humans? It cannot be consciousness alone, since Teilhard has made this a feature of the whole universe. He says:

> If we wish to settle this question of the 'superiority' of man over the animals . . . I can only see one way of doing so – to brush resolutely aside all those secondary and equivocal manifestations of inner activity in human behaviour, making straight for the central phenomenon, *reflection*.[27]

Reflection is the ability of consciousness to turn in upon itself and to know itself. As he goes on to say, 'Admittedly the animal knows. *But it cannot know it knows:* that is quite certain.'[28] What happened is that

> By a tiny 'tangential' increase, the 'radial' was turned back on itself and so to speak took an infinite leap forward.[29]

This leap forward is the move from instinct to thought, and it results, on the individual level, in *hominization*, the appearance of persons. On the corporate level Teilhard talks about *noogenesis* (the coming into being of mind), which leads to the development of a *noosphere*. This is a 'mind layer' which envelops the Earth, just as the lithosphere (rock layer), hydrosphere (water layer), atmosphere (gas layer) and biosphere (life layer) do. Because the Earth is spherical, as the noosphere grows it 'turns in on itself', just as consciousness does in the individual's act of reflection.

In humans evolution becomes aware of itself. This puts humans in a unique position. They are at the head of the whole movement of evolution, and must accept this fact and take up the cosmic responsibility that goes with it. This means doing the utmost to forward their own evolution. To do this we must know that a suitable outcome of evolution is possible. What might this be? Teilhard says that two paths are possible: a divergent or a convergent one. A divergent path would lead to a state of diffusion of consciousness, and Teilhard more or less dismisses this possibility. By contrast, a convergent path will lead to a definite point or state of integration where all consciousnesses will converge: the *Omega Point*. Teilhard speaks as if this were an inevitable outcome of evolution:

> All our difficulties . . . would be dissipated if only we understood that, by structure, the noosphere (and more generally the world) represent a whole

that is not only closed but also *centred*. Because it contains and engenders consciousness, space-time is necessarily of a *convergent nature*. Accordingly its enormous layers, followed in the right direction, must somewhere ahead become involuted to a point which we call *Omega*, which fuses and consumes them integrally in itself.[30]

At the Omega Point the whole universe becomes personalized; indeed it becomes the *Hyper-Personal*.

Now, although all that has been said so far may seem to imply that the Omega Point lies in the (distant) future, Teilhard argues that it is also a present reality. He reaches this conclusion for negative reasons: if it is to be the goal of evolution, it must exist now in order to give us the motivation to strive for the survival and further evolution of the human race. Thus he says:

> To be supremely attractive, Omega must be supremely present . . . To satisfy the ultimate requirements of our action, Omega must be independent of the collapse of the forces with which evolution is woven.[31]

He describes Omega as being not only the last term of its series, but as also being outside all series. Although it emerges from the rise and convergence of consciousness, it has already emerged; it has escaped from the time and space and biosphere that produced it.

This brings us to the end of the 'scientific' section of *The Phenomenon of Man*. It is followed by a short epilogue on 'The Christian Phenomenon'. In this Teilhard identifies God, the Centre of centres, with the Omega Point of evolution. He presents evolution as a process which takes place under the lordship of Christ. Through the incarnation Christ has assumed the control and leadership of evolution and is in a position

> . . . to purify, to direct and superanimate the general ascent of consciousness into which he inserted himself . . . And when he has gathered everything together and transformed everything, he will close in upon himself and his conquests, thereby rejoining, in a final gesture, the divine focus he has never left.[32]

This leads Teilhard to say that the Christogenesis of the New Testament, the summing up of all things in Christ of which St Paul speaks, is the extension of noogenesis in which cosmogenesis culminates. He seems to equate the mystical body of Christ with this final state of the cosmos when he says that then 'Christ invests himself organically with the very majesty of his creation'.[33]

The attraction of Teilhard for New Agers

The attraction of Teilhard's thought for New Agers should now be fairly obvious. His view of reality is essentially monistic. Any dualism of matter and mind or spirit is removed by his concept of the within and without in all forms of matter, and his equating of all forms of energy with psychic energy. The drawing of all things together in the Omega Point removes any rigid distinction between God and humans, indeed between God and the whole cosmos.

Teilhard himself was sensitive to the charge that he was a pantheist. He responds to this briefly in an appendix at the end of *The Phenomenon of Man*. In it he says that his view is

> . . . a very real 'pantheism' if you like (in the etymological meaning of the word) but an absolutely legitimate pantheism – for if, in the last resort, the reflective centres of the world are effectively no more than 'one with God', this state is obtained not by identification (God becoming all) but by the differentiating and communicating action of love (God becoming all *in everyone*). And that is essentially orthodox and Christian.[34]

Whether it is orthodox and Christian is debatable. What he says about God and the Omega Point can be interpreted in a fairly orthodox way.[35] He certainly stresses that the Omega Point is separate from, and transcends, the evolving cosmos. It may be this that leads Capra to say that Teilhard's view of God needs to be 'liberated from its patriarchal connotations'.[36] What Teilhard says about God as the Omega Point does, however, leave the way open to a pantheistic interpretation of God as the directing life force of the universe, or as

Capra puts it, 'the universal dynamics of self-organization'.[37]

The idea of evolution passing through critical points, major leaps forward, is also one that is amenable to New Age interpretation. Marilyn Ferguson appeals to this aspect of Teilhard's teaching to give credence to her claim that humanity is going through such a period now, with a great expansion and change in its consciousness.[38] She also draws support from what he says about the need for humans to grasp the truth that they can now control their own evolution and to take this responsibility seriously. His stress on the need for co-operation and love in order to bring about the convergence of the noosphere is exactly the message she too wants to convey.

Teilhard's view of evil was what got him into trouble with his superiors in the Society of Jesus. Perhaps because of that, there is no systematic treatment of the problem of evil anywhere in his writings. In December 1917 he noted in his diary that he was planning a study that would cover all the major aspects of evil.[39] However, that study never materialized. He does discuss the topic in a brief appendix to *The Phenomenon of Man*.[40] Here, evil is presented as basically the tendency of the products of evolution to decompose or to develop in directions which preclude further advance. Teilhard speaks of this as a necessary aspect of the evolutionary process, as 'relentlessly imposed by the play of large numbers at the heart of a multitude undergoing organisation'. The implication of this seems to be that, as the forces of disintegration are overcome as the cosmos approaches the Omega Point, evil will naturally disappear. This may be what led Teilhard to write on one occasion:

> In our modern perspectives of a universe in the state of cosmogenesis, how is it that so many intelligent people obstinately refuse to see that, intellectually speaking, the famous problem *no longer exists*?[41]

In the appendix to *The Phenomenon of Man*, he asks whether there might not be a 'certain excess' of evil over and above that due to 'the normal effect of evolution' that might be due to 'some catastrophe or primordial deviation'. However, he then says, 'On this question, in all loyalty, I do not feel I am in a position to take a stand.' Smith has no doubt that by 'original sin' (a phrase not used in *The Phenomenon of Man*) Teilhard did mean the disorder and disunion in the evolutionary process that are there even in its earliest phases, and that he failed to make clear how he saw this related to the fall of humans.[42]

Taking simply what is said in *The Phenomenon of Man*, one can see how it can be interpreted in a way that fits in with the non-moral view of evil held by many New Age thinkers and their understanding of the answer to the problem. If evil is the disunion inherent in the evolutionary process up to now, and we humans are now in a position to control evolution, what is needed is for us to realize this truth and act on it. As a result, transformation of the cosmos and the elimination of evil will follow. What Teilhard says in the Foreword to *The Phenomenon of Man* resonates well with such an outlook.[43] Here he speaks of the importance of adopting a new way of *seeing* ourselves in the light of evolution so that we grasp our position as the 'axis and leading shoot of evolution'. It is not surprising that Ferguson includes Teilhard among those who 'describe transformation as new *seeing*'.[44]

Finally, Teilhard's future vision of a state of peace and harmony brought about by the convergence of like minds co-operating in love exactly matches the New Age vision of the Age of Aquarius. No wonder New Agers see him as one of their prophets.

A recent commentator on the New Age sums up the importance of Teilhard for the development of the movement in this way:

> The children of the 1960s counter-culture read de Chardin through the grid of their own experience, and it seemed to them that their intuition was being confirmed by a scientist. They thought that de Chardin's conclusion was that man was indeed in a process of becoming God the Creator. Or, as de Chardin himself put it, humanity was about to become the body of Christ. The process of evolution was about to take its final leap, to meet its destiny by transforming consciousness into super-consciousness; utopia was just around the corner.[45]

6

A CRITIQUE OF
THE PHENOMENON OF MAN

For New Age thinkers, the main attraction of appealing to Teilhard seems to be that he was a scientist (they stress his eminence in geology and palaeontology). Because of this we will take seriously his claim that *The Phenomenon of Man* must be read 'not as a work of metaphysics, still less as a sort of theological essay, but purely and simply as a scientific treatise',[1] and critique it primarily on that level.

The response of scientists to the publication of *The Phenomenon of Man* in 1955 was strongly polarized. Sir Julian Huxley wrote the Introduction to the English edition. In it he endorses most of the central ideas, with the exception of the Omega Point, and describes the book as 'a remarkable success'.[2] On the other hand, Peter Medawar was of the opinion that 'the greater part of the book is nonsense, tricked out by a variety of metaphysical conceits'.[3] There is little doubt that some of the very negative reaction arose because people took Teilhard at his word when he claimed that the book is a 'scientific treatise', and then judged it by *their* understanding of science, which, as we shall see, differed from Teilhard's. F. A. Turk sums the situation up well when he says:

> If we accept Popper's definition of a scientific statement as one capable of disproof then possibly not more than one eighth of the book's statements are, in this sense, scientific.[4]

Most working scientists, whether or not they have heard of Karl Popper and his philosophy of science, do accept something like his definition in their daily work. In his own professional geological and palaeontological articles Teilhard worked on this basis too.[5] Moreover, having said that the book is 'a scientific treatise', near the end of it he admits that one of its central affirmations, that evolution has a direction, is 'strictly undemonstrable to science'.[6] What are we to make of this?

It is important to note that Teilhard makes a distinction between two stages in science: the lower and preliminary stage of *analytical investigation*, and the second stage of *synthesis*.[7] One passes from one stage to the other when the analytical approach to investigation yields no further information on a particular topic. When this happens one inevitably leaves the realm of observation and experiment. As Teilhard puts it, 'Neither in its impetus nor its achievements can science go to its limits without becoming tinged with mysticism and charged with faith.'[8] As we have seen, for Teilhard, that faith involves a belief in the progress and ultimate success of evolution, success being defined in terms of convergence to the Omega Point. It also involves belief in the uniqueness of humans and their pre-eminent place in the evolutionary process, and the conviction that everything must be united in a coherent whole without dualisms such as that of matter and spirit. In the light of these and other beliefs, Teilhard interprets, and builds on, the results of 'analytical science' to produce his all-embracing vision of cosmogenesis. Yet in the 'building' process Teilhard still rests to some extent on observation of 'the phenomenon of man'. He is trying to take into account something of the reality of the way things are. That is probably why, in his view, what he is doing is still in a sense *science*. As Gareth Jones puts it, he is bringing out 'what he believes is implicit in the real, without being limited by a rigid scientific methodology'.[9] Thus Teilhard puts forward the concept of the 'within' of all matter as scientific. This is because his concept begins with the observation that humans have the 'without' of a material body and the 'within' of consciousness, and proceeds by logical deduction. In the process he brings in the two presuppositions of the place of humans at the (current) apex of evolution, and the fundamental oneness of all things.

What is happening here is that Teilhard is using the word 'science' in a very loose way to cover two different ways of reasoning. His 'synthetic' science draws in elements of the metaphysics and theology that he denies the book is about. As a result the book is not simply a 'scientific treatise', as most people would understand that phrase, but *a philosophical and theological interpretation of the scientific evidence.* Teilhard himself was aware of this:

> There is no fact which exists in pure isolation . . . every experience, however objective it may seem, inevitably becomes enveloped in a complex of assumptions as soon as the scientist attempts to explain it. But while this aura of subjective interpretation may remain imperceptible where the field of observation is limited, it is bound to become practically dominant as soon as the field of vision extends to the whole.[10]

What he says here about the impossibility of separating facts from interpretation is true, and widely recognized in the philosophy of science. It does seem useful, however, to draw a line somewhere between the stage where the element of subjective interpretation is 'imperceptible' and the stage where it is dominant, and to reserve the term 'science' for the former stage only. This is because, although there may be a continuum from one extreme to the other, at either end the enterprises one is engaged in are very different.

It is interesting, and surely significant, that those eminent scientists who welcomed *The Phenomenon of Man*, such as Sir Julian Huxley and Joseph Needham,[11] each held an evolutionary world-view that amounted to a 'religion', even if it was a materialistic one. As in Teilhard's case, this formed the basis of their detailed thinking about the meaning and purpose of life. They found Teilhard's overall vision attractive and were not too concerned about its scientific precision. New Age thinkers also find his vision attractive, but then trade on its claimed 'scientific' nature to give added intellectual prestige to their own world-view. Unfortunately this impresses people who have never read Teilhard and do not realize that what he means by science is not what they understand by it.

Another reason many biologists have reacted negatively to Teilhard's views is that his understanding of the mechanism of evolution departed markedly from neo-Darwinian orthodoxy. In *The Phenomenon of Man* he explicitly rejects the neo-Darwinian view that evolutionary change is due solely to random genetic mutations and natural selection.[12] In his view random mutations do play a genuine role in evolution.[13] They provide the raw material of new opportunities to the organism, which makes a 'groping utilization of favourable cases' so that life proceeds by 'strokes of chance which are recognized and grasped – that is to say psychically selected'. As a result the real driving force in evolution is not 'external forces but psychology'. By 'psychology' here he means the driving force of the radial energy of the organism's 'within'. Now Teilhard does not adopt this position on the basis of any appeal to empirical evidence. In fact he omits any discussion of genetics and the contemporary debates about the mechanism of evolution, on the ground that 'these questions do not concern me directly'.[14] It seems that the reason they do not concern him is that his presuppositions have already settled the issue, as the following quotation shows:

> The impetus of the world, glimpsed in the great drive of consciousness, can only have its ultimate source in some *inner* principle, which alone could explain its irreversible advance towards *higher* psychisms.[15]

The 'can only' here is conditioned not by any empirical scientific evidence, but by Teilhard's own anti-dualist metaphysical position.

Teilhard realized that his view would provoke criticism, and specifically the criticism that he was 'showing too Lamarckian a bent'.[16] Lamarck was a forerunner of Darwin. He maintained that an animal's organs develop through use and that these acquired changes are passed on to its offspring. His view found few supporters in his lifetime. From time to time Lamarck's view has been revived in modified forms, but has always failed to gain acceptance because of the absence of clear evidence of the inheritance of acquired characteristics. The similarity between Teilhard's position and classic Lamarckianism is in the idea that the needs or desires of the organism control the acquisition of new characteristics. Lamarck saw this coming about through the use of particular organs (*e.g.* the giraffe's desire for food leading to the stretching of its neck to reach leaves higher up a tree). For Teilhard the inner urge of the organism for development in a particular direction, the acquiring of a greater degree of consciousness, leads to the selection of certain mutations. The common ground, which leads Teilhard to be regarded as a neo-Lamarckian rather than a neo-Darwinian, is the idea of the course of evolution being directed along a straight line by some inner force. Teilhard tried to have the best of both worlds by claiming that he accepted Darwinism in the lower forms of life, whereas Lamarckianism operates in the higher forms.

One can make at least two criticisms with regard to the logic of Teilhard's proposed mechanism for evolution. The first is that if there really are what he calls 'two zones' of evolution, with different mechanisms at work in them, surely the transition from one (the Darwinian) to the other (the Lamarckian) was a very chancy affair. It might well not have happened. This goes against his vision of the whole process as a slow but inexorable ascent towards complexity and consciousness. Secondly, in what way can an organism utilize or not utilize a mutation that occurs in its genes? Can it neutralize a harmful one and not pass it on to its offspring? How does Teilhard envisage the internal selection force of radial energy replacing the external pressure of natural selection?

Teilhard's concept of critical points has also come under criticism. Jones comments:

A critical point is a feature of the 'within', and may be accompanied by no discernible change in the 'without'. The initiative lies with Teilhard's followers to demonstrate the value of this hypothesis for evolutionary thinking, as it corresponds to no demonstrable evidence.[17]

Arthur Peacocke argues for an understanding of the emergence of consciousness that is different from Teilhard's, and in the view of many scientists far more satisfactory in the way in which it rests on the available evidence.[18] The argument is too lengthy and too detailed to reproduce briefly. The essence of the conclusion is that the natural world consists of a hierarchy of organized systems at various levels of complexity. The interacting units at one level form the individual, more complex, units of the next level. Complex biological molecules, for instance, combine to form living cells, and single cells combine to form multi-cellular organisms. At each new level of complexity genuinely new phenomena emerge, for example the genetic code that appears when nucleic acids combine to form the complex DNA molecule. Peacocke sees consciousness as just such an emergent phenomenon. It is not something which exists in an attenuated form in the less complex forms of matter. When the central nervous system reaches a certain level of complexity it appears *de novo*. It is not an 'added extra', but a new property that appears at that level of complexity. A parallel can be drawn with a property such as 'wetness'. The logic of Teilhard's position would require that some attenuated form of 'wetness' exists in the atoms of oxygen and hydrogen, since they combine to form 'wet' water. Indeed, it must also exist in an even more attenuated form in the sub-atomic particles which constitute atoms (why then are only some combinations of atoms 'wet'?). It seems much more reasonable to see 'wetness' as an emergent property that appears only when atoms combine in certain ways.

The Law of Complexity-Consciousness plays a vital role in Teilhard's scheme. N. M. Wildiers says:

> It is this law that in his view affords us the key to a correct view of evolution – which in its turn is a central phenomenon, apart from which the universe cannot be integrated.[19]

So how firmly based is this law? That the evolutionary process has led to increasingly intricate mechanisms and a greater richness of internal organization in organisms is an observable fact. This includes an increase in the complexity of nervous systems, which reaches a climax in humans, who are self-conscious beings. Teilhard assumes that the two processes of increasing physical complexity and rising psychism are inextricably linked throughout the process. This cannot be scientifically demonstrated since psychism cannot be associated with any structural entity in plants and non-living matter. This raises the question why it should be linked with a structural entity, the nervous system, in animals. Far from being a normal scientific law, the Law of

Complexity-Consciousness is an interpretation of trends in the evolutionary process in the light of Teilhard's basic metaphysical commitments.

Without this law, Teilhard could not have made his extrapolation of the future progress of evolution towards the Omega Point. This assumes that evolution will continue as before, but as a psychosocial process rather than a biological one. There is no justification in strict scientific terms for this assumption. All that can be observed as of now are the results of the biological process. With the appearance of humans who are able to control their own development, evolution, at least in their case, passes from being genetically based to being largely non-genetically based. So, any predictions which might be founded on observation of evolution in pre-human creatures are not relevant to human evolutionary development. The Law of Complexity-Consciousness enables Teilhard to take this radical break in the evolutionary process in his stride and make predictions about the future which he claims are 'scientific', in his sense of the term.

Throughout *The Phenomenon of Man* Teilhard stresses that he is seeking to develop a unified and coherent view of reality. However, even some of those who are very sympathetic to the book, such as Sir Julian Huxley,[20] find his idea of the Omega Point unclear, even incoherent. How can Omega be both an emergent future entity and yet be present now? To say that it is both the last term of its series and yet outside all series is surely to introduce into his system just the kind of dualism that he has tried to avoid all along. Huxley is right to see that what is happening here is a 'gallant attempt' to reconcile a (more or less) orthodox Christian concept of God with a system of thought that would logically lead to a finite god who is complete only at the end of the course of development of the universe.

Finally, it is surprising that in a scheme that claims to take 'the phenomenon of man' seriously as its starting-point, Teilhard has nothing to say about the fact that humans are characteristically not just 'reflective' beings, but also 'religious' beings.

Since there is little explicit theology in *The Phenomenon of Man*, it is neither necessary nor appropriate to attempt any detailed critique of Teilhard's theology. There is no doubt about his desire to remain as close as he could to an orthodox Roman Catholic position. As we have seen, he even sacrifices the coherence of his grand system to achieve this with regard to the Omega Point, understood as God. The result is no more satisfactory from a Christian point of view than it is from a scientific one. As R. B. Smith, another sympathizer, has to admit, 'With regard to the doctrine of God, his ideas raise more questions than they answer.'[21] Teilhard clearly wants his scheme to be Christocentric. He makes Christ the Lord of the evolutionary process. However, it is hard, in terms of the logic of Teilhard's scheme, to see why Christ needed to enter into the process in an 'incarnation' in order to adopt this role. While there is emphasis on the cosmic Christ, the place of the redemptive Christ is not clear. This follows from the lack of any clear doctrine of evil. If evil is solely, or even primarily, an inherent 'disorder' in the evolutionary process then, as we have seen, it will disappear naturally as the process converges to the Omega Point. There seems to be no need for the cross. Moreover, the logic of the scheme means that, as far as it implies a 'doctrine of salvation', it must be universalistic in outlook. In fact, salvation ultimately seems to depend on the efforts of humankind in directing evolution towards convergence rather than divergence. Human socialization is what leads to divinization at the Omega Point.

Conclusion

We have seen how and why Teilhard's optimistic, monistic, evolutionary vision is attractive to New Age thinkers. It can be readily adapted to accord with their ideology. For those who want the respectability derived from claiming the support of science for their position, Teilhard has the added attraction of having been a notable scientist who presented his vision as one firmly based on science. We have seen that that claim is flawed, both because it rests on an idiosyncratic definition of science, and because Teilhard's vision implies a view of the evolutionary process which is at odds with that of modern evolutionary biologists. The vision itself runs into incoherence when Teilhard tries to wed it to an orthodox Christian understanding of reality.

7

BIOLOGY AND NEW AGE THOUGHT

Although New Age thinkers usually adopt an optimistic evolutionary framework of thought, there has been no detailed attempt to relate New Age ideology to modern biology in the way that has been done with modern physics. We will consider a short discussion of biology and New Age thought by Fritjof Capra and then discuss the work of Rupert Sheldrake, which has attracted the interest of many New Agers.

A systems view of life[1]

Capra criticizes contemporary biology for its Cartesian, mechanistic approach to the understanding of living organisms. It reduces their functioning to cellular and molecular mechanisms. He accepts that there is some validity to this approach, but protests against the assumption that its apparent success justifies regarding living organisms as machines. Instead he argues for a fuller understanding of living organisms by developing a 'systems biology' that sees an organism as a living system rather than a machine. This stresses relationships and integration rather than the individual parts that make up the system.

According to Capra there are four main aspects to a systems view:[2]

1. Systems are seen as integrated wholes that are more than the sum

of their parts. Their properties cannot be reduced to those of the smaller units which make up the system.

2. This leads to an emphasis on the basic principles of organization, rather than the basic building blocks or substances, of the system.

3. An important basic principle of organization is a process known as transaction – 'the simultaneous and mutually interdependent inter-action between multiple components'.[3]

4. Systems are intrinsically dynamic in nature. Their forms are not rigid structures but are flexible yet stable manifestations of underlying processes.

Capra argues that living systems have two particular characteristics. First, they are self-organizing systems.[4] Their order in structure and function is not imposed by the environment but is established by the system itself. As a result they exhibit a certain degree of autonomy. This is not to say that they are isolated from their environment. They interact with it continually, but this interaction does not determine their organization.

Secondly, living systems form multi-levelled structures whose levels differ in their complexity.[5] At each level of complexity the systems are integrated, self-organizing wholes which are made up of smaller parts, but at the same time act as parts of larger wholes. The human organism, made up as it is of various organs, each organ made up of tissues and each tissue made up of cells, is an example of this.

A Christian can agree whole-heartedly with Capra's protest against a purely mechanistic, reductionist approach to biology. We have already argued, in our discussion of physics (see pages 58–60 above) that there is evidence from within science of the limitations of a reductionist methodology, and that the whole *is* more than the sum of its parts. From a specifically Christian perspective, any account of reality in general, and human beings in particular, that limits itself to a materialistic, mechanistic viewpoint will inevitably be incomplete and distorted because it ignores a vital aspect of reality, the spiritual dimension.

Having said that, problems do arise when Capra tries to derive metaphysical implications from his systems view of life. For example, he argues that 'the relative autonomy of self-organizing systems sheds new light on the age-old philosophical question of free will'.[6] It must be said that this light will appear to many as neither particularly new nor very illuminating. His argument amounts to saying that a system is free to the extent that it is autonomous from its environment – which seems a truism. Capra goes on to claim that the relative autonomy of organisms usually increases with their complexity, and reaches its culmination in human beings. This can, perhaps, be seen as a specific insight from his systems approach. However, while it is relevant to that aspect of the free will/determinism debate that has been concerned with the influence of the environment on human freedom, it does not touch the theological aspect of the debate, that between Arminians and Calvinists. Capra also claims that the relative concept of free will that arises in a systems view of life is consistent with certain mystical traditions that exhort their followers to transcend the notion of an isolated self, and to become aware that they are inseparable parts of the cosmos. Once such a state is reached, he says,

> The question of free will seems to lose its meaning. If I *am* the universe, there can be no 'outside' influences and all my actions will be spontaneous and free. From the point of view of mystics, therefore, the notion of free will is relative, limited and – as they would say – illusory, like all other concepts we use in our rational descriptions of reality.[7]

There seems to be some woolly thinking here. From a systems point of view, the fact that I am the universe does not necessarily evacuate the question of free will of any meaning. When arguing for a systems view of life Capra spends some time distinguishing between machines and organisms. It would seem reasonable to ask the question whether the universe is a machine or an organism, and to see a machine-type universe as one that has no free will, while an organism-type universe does have some free will since, as Capra argues, an organism is self-organizing in a way that a machine is not. Whatever else a systems view of life does, it does not lend support to the view that free will is an illusory concept. Capra seems to make an illegitimate equation between the idea of relative freedom in systems theory and the idea of the relativity of free will that he finds in the views of some mystics.

Biology and physics

Capra claims that a systems approach to biology reveals that two concepts that have arisen in sub-atomic physics also apply to living systems. These are ideas that have importance for his attempt to relate the mystical view of reality with modern physics.

As we have seen, Capra stresses that living systems are multi-levelled structures with levels that differ in complexity. In the human body, for instance, we can think in terms of individual cells which combine to form tissues. Various tissues combine to form organs (for example the stomach or the lungs). These organs form different organ systems (such as the digestive system or the respiratory system). Finally, the organ systems taken together form the organism we call a human being. Systems theorists would normally call this kind of organization 'hierarchical'. Capra, however, dislikes that term because of its authoritarian overtones, and speaks instead of a 'systems tree':

> As a real tree takes its nourishment through both its roots and its leaves, so the power in a systems tree flows in both directions, with neither end dominating the other and all levels interacting in interdependent harmony to support the functioning of the whole.[8]

Following P. A. Weiss,[9] Capra asserts that the division of systems into levels is not something inherent in the system, but really a matter of the level of the observer's attention. Therefore, he says,

> The new insight of subatomic physics also seems to hold for the study of living matter: the observed patterns of matter are reflections of patterns of mind.[10]

In some cases of systems analysis there is no doubt a measure of truth in this claim. However, at least some of the distinctions of levels do have an objective basis in the system rather than being simply imposed by the observer. This is surely the case with single cells or discrete organs such as the pancreas. Even the distinction between different organic systems, although more fuzzy since the systems may interact or overlap, has a basis in the functioning of the systems, not just in the mind of the observer.

The other parallel that Capra draws with modern physics is

> . . . the fact that the notion of complementarity, which was so crucial in the development of atomic physics, also seems to play an important role in the new systems biology.[11]

What Capra is referring to here is the fact that in living systems there are 'complementary tendencies' which are in 'continual dynamic interplay'. For example, there is the interplay between 'self-assertive and integrative tendencies' and between 'self-maintenance' and 'self-transformation and self-transcendence'. Here, however, some sloppy semantics is at work. In quantum physics 'complementarity' has a very specific meaning. It refers to the need to use logically incompatible mathematical models in order to describe the whole range of behaviour of a system. The incompatible models can never be used together. Each is used in specific situations. However, what Capra is talking about with regard to living systems is quite different. Here he uses the word 'complementary' more or less in the way it is used in ordinary speech, in which a 'complement' is 'something which completes a whole'.[12] Moreover, the tendencies he refers to, and as he defines them, are not logically incompatible. Thus, by 'self-maintenance' he means such things as the ability to heal wounds, to respond to environmental stresses such as changes in temperature or altitude, and reproduction. This is by no means logically incompatible with the 'self-transcendence' of a series developing new patterns of behaviour or new structures.

It is not clear what Capra is trying to establish by these supposed parallels between quantum physics and biology. Since he frequently draws a contrast between 'classical science' and the systems view of living organisms, he may be intending to associate systems theory with the prestige of non-classical physics. Whatever his aim may be, he fails to achieve it because, as we argued, the parallels he draws are illegitimate.

A systems view of evolution

Basing himself on the work of E. Jantsch,[13] Capra argues that a systems-theory approach provides a better understanding of evolution than does neo-Darwinism. He sums up the essence of this approach as follows:

> The basic dynamics of evolution, according to the new systems view, begins with a system in homeostasis – a state of dynamic balance characterized by multiple, inter-dependent fluctuations. When the system is disturbed it has the tendency to maintain its stability by means of negative feedback mechanisms, which tend to reduce the deviation from the balanced state. However, this is not the only possibility. Deviations may also be reinforced internally through positive feedback, either in response to environmental changes or spontaneously without external influence. The stability of living systems is continually tested by its fluctuations, and at certain moments one or several of them may become so strong that they drive the system over an instability into an entire new structure, which will again be fluctuating and relatively stable.[14]

He argues that this differs from the classical neo-Darwinian outlook in two ways.

1. The classical theory concentrates on movement towards an equilibrium state, with organisms becoming ever more perfectly adapted to their environment. If this were the core of evolution, he says, it is hard to explain why living forms ever evolved beyond the blue-green algae, which are perfectly adapted to their environment and are very successful reproductively. According to the systems view, evolution operates far from equilibrium and unfolds through the interplay of adaptation and creativity.

2. The classical theory focuses on the evolution of the organism as it adapts to an environment that changes independently of it, whereas the systems view focuses on the co-evolution of organism plus environment.

There is considerable justice in Capra's second point. However, his first point is open to challenge. The answer to his point about the blue-green algae is that there has always been only a finite amount of habitat that was ideal for this species. Once this was all occupied, any mutation that would allow the colonization of a slightly different habitat would lead to evolution in a new direction. This also raises the question of what Capra means by 'creativity', if by it he means anything other than genetic mutations. In fact, his description of evolution according to a systems view sounds impressive, but it lacks specificity. What does he mean by 'fluctuations' or 'deviations . . . reinforced internally through positive feedback' when applied to a specific organism or species? Unless he means something other than genetic diversity and mutation we are back with neo-Darwinism.

According to Capra:

> In the systems view the process of evolution is not dominated by 'blind chance' but represents an unfolding of order and complexity that can be seen as a kind of learning process, involving autonomy and freedom of choice.[15]

What does he mean here by 'freedom of choice'? He says that when a system becomes unstable, there are always at least two new possible structures into which it can evolve. He then asserts:

> Which of these options is chosen is impossible to predict; there is true freedom of choice. As the system approaches the critical point, it 'decides' itself which way to go, and this decision will determine its evolution.[16]

Two points are notable here. First, freedom of choice is equated with unpredictability. This is strange, since if a human being constantly behaves in an unpredictable way it is usually taken as evidence of mental instability and that person needs some kind of medical treatment. Rational behaviour may be perfectly free, yet is often predictable to other rational beings. Secondly, the use of quotation marks here shows that Capra is aware of using the word 'decide' in a figurative way. However, from then on he drops the quotation marks and seems to intend his talk of systems 'deciding' and 'choosing' to be taken literally. In other words, he performs a semantic sleight of hand which seems to deceive him, if not his readers. To appreciate this we need only consider in what way a non-human system can be said to decide its evolutionary path.

When the proliferation of factories covered the vegetation of parts of England with soot it upset the equilibrium between the peppered moth and its predators. The light-coloured moth was no longer well camouflaged when it settled on a tree. It was easily spotted by its predators. What possible 'new structures' could arise from this non-equilibrium situation? Presumably, the moth could have become extinct, or its predators could have lost their taste for it, or the moth's colouring could change. In what sense did an individual moth or predator have any choice in the outcome? None, as far as we know. Moreover, despite Capra's assertion, the outcome was predictable. The genotype of the moth was not uniform, a small proportion of the population always having a darker than average colouring. These darker moths (whether they chose to like it or not) were now quite well camouflaged and so survived to lay eggs which produced more dark-coloured moths, and so the species survived but with the balance of colour in the population changed. A new equilibrium had been established.

Capra says that the new systems theory of evolution rules out both the scientific view that reduces evolution to a cosmic game of dice, and the religious view that there is some general blueprint. The basis for this claim is his assertion that systems have freedom of choice. The 'freedom' aspect rules out the divine blueprint and the 'choice' rules out the chance element. If, as argued above, talk of 'freedom of choice' is a semantic sleight of hand, then the claim falls to the ground.

While denying that there is any divine blueprint for the course of evolution, Capra does say that a general pattern can be recognized in the process. The characteristics of this pattern include

> . . . the progressive increase of complexity, coordination and interdepend-
> ence; the integration of individuals into multileveled systems; and the
> continual refinement of certain functions and patterns of behavior.[17]

A systems view of mind, consciousness and God

Capra's talk of systems 'deciding' which path to follow makes some kind of sense in terms of his redefinition of the meaning of mind and mental activity. As he puts it:

> From the systems point of view, life is not a substance or a force, and mind is not an entity interacting with matter. Both life and mind are manifestations of the same set of systemic properties, a set of processes that represent the dynamics of self-organization.[18]

According to this definition all living organisms have a mind. However, Capra does make a distinction between 'mind', a term he uses for organisms of high complexity, and what he calls 'mentation', the dynamics of self-organization at lower levels. He goes on to say:

> The description of mind as a pattern of organization, or a set of dynamic relationships, is related to the description of matter in modern physics. Mind and matter no longer appear to belong to two fundamentally separate categories, as Descartes believed, but can be seen to represent merely different aspects of the same universal process.[19]

Once again we have a very questionable appeal to ideas in modern physics. It is questionable for two reasons. First of all, it is probable that what Capra has in mind here is the so-called 'bootstrap theory' of sub-atomic particles, which regards them as composed of one another in such a way that each of them involves all the others. This theory was falling out of favour at the time Capra wrote his book, and has very few supporters today. Secondly, even if what Capra is referring to is quantum field theory, which is widely held and which describes sub-atomic particles in terms of energy fields, it is quite illegitimate simply to equate these energy fields implicitly with the 'pattern of organiza-tion' of a living system which Capra calls 'mind', and then to say that mind and matter are merely different aspects of the same thing.

Discussion of consciousness is not helped by the fact that different people use the term to mean different things. Capra is careful to define what he means by it. His definition of mind means that it is a property that is widely spread. However, he says:

> Self-awareness, on the other hand, seems to manifest itself only in higher animals, unfolding fully in the human mind, and it is this property of mind that I mean by consciousness.[20]

He goes on to argue that most theories about the nature of consciousness can be seen as variations on one of two opposing views. These are the Western scientific view and the mystical view.

The scientific view considers matter as primary, and sees consciousness as a property of complex material patterns that emerges at a certain stage of evolution. The mystical view regards consciousness as the primary reality and ground of all being. According to this view 'pure consciousness' is non-material, formless and void of content. The mystical view is based on the experience of reality in non-ordinary states of awareness, traditionally achieved through meditation. The mystics claim that in these experiences they make contact with a collective, even a cosmic, consciousness. Capra argues that, because at present these experiences lie outside of the reality which science can investigate, science does not contradict the mystical view of consciousness, while not confirming it. In fact, in his view, the systems approach provides a framework for bringing the two opposing views together. The systems view agrees with the scientific view that consciousness is a manifestation of complex material patterns. It is a manifestation of living systems of a certain complexity. On the other hand, the biological structures of these systems express the system's self-organization, and so its mind. In this sense material structures are not the primary reality. Extrapolating this to the universe as a whole leads to the conclusion that all its structures are manifestations of the universe's self-organizing dynamics, which can be regarded as the cosmic mind. This is close to the mystical view. So, concludes Capra,

> The systems view of nature at last seems to provide a meaningful scientific framework for approaching the age-old questions of the nature of life, mind, consciousness and matter.[21]

This sweeping conclusion is very questionable. In the heart of Capra's systems view of life lies a major unanswered question. He can claim that his view brings together mind and matter because of the fact that he defines mind and matter as different aspects of the set of processes that represent the dynamics of the self-organization of the universe. But what is the nature of those processes? Where does the self-organization spring from? Without a clear answer to these questions, the out-and-out materialist will not accept his demotion of matter to a mere 'aspect' of these processes of an undefined nature. At the same time the mystics can, with some justice, claim that Capra has really joined their side against the conventional scientific view.

The justice of the mystics' claim would lie in what Capra says about God in relation to a systems view of life. In the light of what he says about the multi-levelled ('systems tree') nature of living organisms, it is not surprising to find him concluding that individual human minds are embedded in the larger minds of social and ecological systems. He explicitly accepts[22] Jung's theory of a collective psyche which includes a collective unconscious mind.[23] These larger minds, he suggests, are integrated into a planetary mental system, which in turn must participate in some kind of universal or cosmic mind. This cosmic mind, he says, does not have to be associated with the traditional idea of God. It 'represents nothing less than the self-organizing dynamics of the entire cosmos'.[24] He quotes with approval the words of Jantsch: 'God is not the creator, but the mind of the universe.'[25]

Here, of course, we have a clearly pantheistic concept of God. Capra may not have associated the cosmic mind of his systems theory with the traditional Judaeo-Christian idea of God, but he has associated it with the traditional pantheistic idea found in Greek Stoicism and various strands of Hinduism and Buddhism.

Conclusion

The motivation behind Capra's systems view of life is a desire to break free from the mechanistic, reductionist approach to living organisms that characterizes conventional biology. From a Christian point of view, the desire to avoid metaphysical (as distinct from merely methodo-logical)[26] reductionism is laudable. Capra's attempt, however, is un-satisfactory for a number of reasons.

First, as we have pointed out a number of times in the exposition of the main features of his approach, there are logical flaws and woolly thinking in his argument. In particular his approach does not provide the answers to such classical problems as the understanding of free will and consciousness that he claims it does.

Secondly, Capra seems to be guilty of a form of reductionism himself. Ultimately he reduces everything to the dynamics of self-organization of the universe. At this point he has only two options. He can either make those dynamics a property of matter, in which case he is back with conventional metaphysical materialism, or he can give those dynamics a metaphysical status of their own, which is a form of pantheism.

In an earlier chapter (see pages 58–63 above) we have argued that trinitarian theism provides a viable alternative metaphysical frame-work to the one adopted by Capra and other New Age thinkers. A view of life that emphasizes the dynamic inter-relatedness of things sits quite comfortably with a metaphysics which grounds everything in an ultimate reality which consists of just such a dynamic set of personal relationships. The difference is that the 'cosmic mind' is not then trapped in the universe, but is God the Spirit not only immanently at work in the created order, but also transcending it. The immanent work of the divine Spirit in the 'normal' process of life is no new idea, but finds expression at various times in the Bible. For example, we read in the book of Job: 'The spirit of God has made me, and the breath of the Almighty gives me life' (Job 33:4). Speaking of all living creatures the psalmist says:

> When thou hidest thy face, they are dismayed;
>> when thou takest away their breath, they die
>> and return to their dust.
> When thou sendest forth thy Spirit [or 'breath', margin], they are created;
>> and thou renewest the face of the ground.

(Psalm 104:29–30)

Note here the poetic play on the double meaning of the Hebrew word *rûaḥ*, 'breath/spirit'. This enables the poet to imply a close link between the 'life force' in living creatures and the activity of the divine Spirit in the created order. The apostle Paul is able to find some common ground with Greek thought when he says, 'Yet he [God] is not far from each one of us, for "in him we live and move and have our being"' (Acts 17:28).[27] Earlier Paul has said that God 'gives to all men life and breath and everything' (Acts 17:25). Paul, a strong theist, rejected the pantheism of the Greek Stoics, but could endorse their insight that God is immanently at work in the cosmos. His God, however, was the Creator God of his Hebrew forebears, now made known in a fuller way through Jesus Christ.

8

A NEW SCIENCE OF LIFE

Lawrence Osborn points out that although adherents of the New Age movement generally claim to be 'holistic' in their thinking, some none the less tend to a dualistic view of mind and matter.[1] They see humans, and other creatures, as made up of a body animated by some life force, or soul. Such a view has proved difficult to relate in any coherent way with modern biological science. This, says Osborn, is why a new holistic approach to biology pioneered by Rupert Sheldrake has been welcomed with enthusiasm by many New Agers. They see it as providing a solution to the problem.

Sheldrake gained a PhD in biochemistry at Cambridge and was a Fellow of Clare College and Director of Studies in biochemistry and cell biology from 1967 to 1973. In 1974 he joined the staff of the International Crops Research Institute for the Semi-Arid Tropics at Hyderabad in India, where he worked on the physiology of tropical legume crops until 1978. He then spent eighteen months at an ashram in Trinchinopoly writing the first draft of his book *A New Science of Life*.

The book provoked considerable controversy when it was published in 1981.[2] The reviews of the book were mixed, but not unfriendly. The general attitude was perhaps summed up by the comment that the book was 'an attractive and sound presentation of an improbable thesis'.[3] However, the editor of the prestigious scientific journal *Nature* wrote an editorial in which he described it as 'this infuriating tract' and said that, although books should not be burned, this one was 'the best candidate for burning there has been for many years'.[4] This intemperate attack helped to keep discussion of the book and its ideas going for several months, not only in scientific journals and magazines, but also in newspapers and on radio and television programmes.

After some years out of the public eye, media interest in the New Age movement, and the interest of New Age thinkers in Sheldrake's ideas, have brought Sheldrake to the attention of the media. He has appeared on several programmes in the role of the scientist who defends some New Age ideas against his orthodox, conservative colleagues. BBC2 television devoted a thirty-minute programme to him in its *Heretic* series on 'unorthodox scientists'.[5] In this programme he was described as someone whose ideas were very attractive to New Agers, from whom he received a lot of support.

Morphogenesis

A large proportion of *A New Science of Life* is taken up with the subject of morphogenesis, the way in which the characteristic and specific form of living organisms comes into being. Sheldrake identifies four different aspects of this problem.[6]

The first is the fact that in the process of development, new structures appear which cannot be explained in terms of the unfolding or growth of structures which are already present in the egg at the beginning of development. The single fertilized cell that is the start of a new human being does not have miniature arms, legs, head and the like that simply increase in size. These features appear as the cells divide and multiply.

The second problem arises from the first. How is the process of development regulated? Why do some groups of developing cells form a liver while others form a leg? Moreover, how is it that if, when an embryo is at the two-cell stage, one cell is destroyed, the other does not develop into half an organism but into a smaller, but complete, organism?

The third problem associated with morphogenesis is that organisms are able to replace or restore damaged structures. Plants show an amazing ability to do this, as anyone who has pruned them knows.

Some invertebrates have striking powers of regeneration. If a flatworm, for example, is cut into pieces, each can regenerate into a complete worm.

The fourth difficulty is that reproduction should not be taken for granted. It is amazing that a detached part of the parent becomes a whole new organism.

Historically, three different types of theory have been proposed to explain morphogenesis: mechanistic, vitalist and organismic. Each can be, and has been, developed into a general approach to the science of life.

The modern mechanistic theory of morphogenesis makes the role of DNA of primary importance. Ultimately, it is believed, everything can be explained in terms of what is 'programmed' into the genes which this very large molecule contains. 'Believed' is the key word here. It is known that the DNA contains the information which controls the production of enzymes in the living cell. These enzymes are proteins which catalyse the chemical reaction taking place in the cell. There are feedback systems which 'switch on' and 'switch off' the synthesis of enzymes controlled by the DNA. Many of the structures in cells have a 'self-assembly' nature arising from their chemical and physical constitution. A great deal of the biochemistry of how cells function has now been elucidated. We still do not know, however, why it is that, although all the cells in the human body have the same DNA, some develop into skin cells, some into nerve cells, and some into muscle cells. Nor is it known why some combine to produce a heart, and others to produce a head. Mechanists believe that these differences depend on physico-chemical patterns within the developing system of cells. Various possibilities have been suggested: concentration gradients of specific chemicals; electrical gradients; or mechanical contacts between cells. How these influences might be 'interpreted' by cells is another dimension of the problem. There is also, of course, the question of where the 'programme' of the DNA came from. Can we really accept that it is the product of purely chance processes? Given the current degree of ignorance, it is easy for sceptics to claim that a totally mechanistic explanation will never be found.

Vitalists believe that the phenomena of life cannot be fully understood in terms of physical laws derived only from the study of inanimate systems, but that an additional causal factor is at work in living organisms. Vitalism was quite widespread in the first half of the nineteenth century. Ideas about it were too vague, however, to offer effective alternatives to the developing mechanistic explanations provided by biochemists as the century progressed. The causal factors proposed – immaterial souls, formative impulses, entelechies (goal-directed influences) – are all considered to be non-material and non-energetic. They cannot be found by dissecting the organism into its material component parts. Their action does not contravene the laws of thermodynamics. As a result, vitalist theories are inherently dualistic. They postulate the existence of factors which scientists could never detect. Consequently it is hard to conceive of any experimental tests of these theories. Most modern biochemists and biologists have therefore ignored them.

Sheldrake uses the term 'organismic' to denote twentieth-century theories of morphogenesis which invoke the idea of 'morphogenetic fields'.[7] These fields, it is proposed, shape and guide the development of the whole organism towards its goal. Like the known fields of physics, these fields are supposed to exist within and around organisms and contain within themselves a nested hierarchy of fields, such as cell fields, tissue fields or organ fields. Analogies have been drawn with magnetic fields. Just as cutting a magnet in two gives rise to two complete magnets, so cutting up organisms like flatworms gives rise to pieces with complete flatworm fields, enabling them to regenerate into flatworms. These ideas arose in the 1920s.

C. H. Waddington extended the idea of the field, which could be taken as a static one, to take into account the temporal aspect of development.[8] He introduced what he called the *chreode* (from two Greek words meaning 'necessary path'). He visualized this in terms of a three-dimensional landscape with series of branching valleys. These represent alternative paths of development for the embryo. In some cases valleys diverge but then reunite. These are alternative ways of reaching the same goal. Other valley systems remain quite separate, representing the development of different organs. If a developing organ is thought of as a ball rolling down a valley, various influences (genetic, environmental) may push it away from the valley bottom up the enclosing hillside, but unless it is pushed over into another valley system, the process of development will find its way back to its goal. It is possible to express such models mathematically.

The status of morphogenetic fields or chreodes is a matter of debate. They can be seen as simply descriptions of the way in which organisms do develop. This is how Waddington seems to have regarded them. If they are regarded as in some sense an explanation of morphogenesis, then they must be causative. In this case, are they fields which are ultimately explicable in terms of known physical principles, or are they of a different nature from the fields currently known to physicists? In the first case we would be dealing with an essentially mechanistic theory. In the second we may be dealing with something different, but is it different from vitalism? It is Sheldrake's claim that he has developed a theory based on morphogenetic fields which is not vitalistic and which is experimentally testable.

Formative causation

Sheldrake proposes that morphogenetic fields play a causal role in the development and maintenance of the forms of organized systems at all levels of complexity, including molecules, crystals, cells, tissues and organisms. 'Form' here 'is taken to include not only the shape of the outer surface or boundary of a system, but also its internal structure'. The causation of form by morphogenetic fields he calls 'formative causation' because he wants

> . . . to distinguish it from the energetic type of causation with which physics already deals so thoroughly. For although morphogenetic fields can only bring about their effects in conjunction with energetic processes, they are not in themselves energetic.[9]

Sheldrake draws an analogy with the plan of a house. This causes the specific form of a house. It is not the only cause. The plan could not be realized without the building materials and the activity of the builders.

However, the plan is the crucial factor which determines the specific form of the house, and yet its contribution to the building is not one of the processes in the building which involve energy changes. Morphogenetic fields can be regarded as analogous to the known fields of physics, such as gravitational and electromagnetic, in that they are capable of ordering physical changes, even though they themselves cannot be observed directly. 'Morphogenetic fields are spatial structures detectable only through their morphogenetic effects on material systems.'[10]

According to the organismic theory, says Sheldrake, all structured systems are made up of smaller organized units. He calls these 'morphic units'. These are arranged in a hierarchical system. A crystal, for example, is made up of molecules, which are made up of atoms, which are made up of sub-atomic particles. This means that

> A higher-level morphic unit must somehow co-ordinate the arrangement of the parts of which it is composed. It will be assumed to do so through the influence of its morphogenetic field on the morphogenetic fields of lower-level morphic units. Thus morphogenetic fields, like morphic units themselves, are essentially hierarchical in their organization.[11]

Morphogenesis can begin only from an already organized system. This acts as a 'morphogenetic germ' by becoming embedded in the morphogenetic field of a large morphic unit. For this to happen the 'germ' must be a characteristic part of that unit. Initially the rest of the unit's field is 'unoccupied', containing only the 'virtual form' of the final system. This form is actualized as the appropriate component parts come within range of the influence of the field and fit into their correct relative positions.[12]

Morphic resonance

The constancy and repetition of natural forms of, for example, a particular species present no problem for the mechanistic theory, since the form is presumed to be uniquely determined by changeless physical laws. Sheldrake recognizes that there is a potential problem here for his theory of formative causation. One solution would be to regard all morphogenetic fields as eternal, inexplicable givens, like Plato's eternal Forms. Sheldrake, however, proposes a radically different solution. According to this,

> Chemical and biological forms are repeated not because they are determined by changeless laws or eternal Forms, but because of a *causal influence from previous similar forms.* This influence would require an action across space *and time* unlike any known type of physical action.[13]

He calls the process by which the forms of a previous system influence the morphogenesis of subsequent similar systems 'morphic resonance', by analogy with the 'sympathetic' vibration of stretched strings in response to appropriate sound waves. He assumes that morphic resonance is not attenuated by either time or space, and that it takes place only from the past.[14]

Of course morphic resonance cannot occur on the first occasion that a particular system comes into being. In Sheldrake's view no *a priori* reason can be given for the form taken up on the initial occasion (for instance, the first time a newly synthesized compound is crystallized from solution).

> The initial choice of a particular form could be ascribed to chance; or to a creativity inherent in matter or to a transcendent creative agency. But there is no way in which these different possibilities could be distinguished from each other by experiment. A decision between them could be made only on metaphysical grounds.[15]

Once this has occurred, however, similar systems will also take up that form because of morphic resonance.

Variability

If an organism develops in accordance with the pre-existing 'template' of a morphogenetic field, why do we see considerable variability

107

between the individual members of a specific species? Sheldrake's answer is first that

> If a particular morphogenetic field is to remain associated with a growing system, then forms must be capable of being 'scaled up' or 'scaled down' within the morphogenetic field. Thus their essential features must depend not on the absolute but the relative positions of their component parts.[16]

Secondly, following Waddington's concept of the chreode, he accepts that there is some room for variability due to environmental and other influences. The result is that there is not just one morphogenetic field for a specific species, but a host of similar fields. As a result,

> . . . morphogenetic fields are not precisely defined but are represented by *probability structures* which depend on the statistical distribution of previous similar forms.[17]

The longer a particular individual organism exists, the more important will be the influence on it of its own past states, with the result that it develops its own specific, stable identity.

Movement, behaviour and learning

Sheldrake argues that there is a close link between morphogenesis, growth and movement. This is most clearly seen in unicellular organisms such as *amoeba*. Such an organism moves by 'growing' projections of its cell (called pseudopodia, 'false feet') in the direction of motion, into which the cytoplasm (the cell fluid) then flows. In multicellular animals, movement depends on the change of form of certain specialized structures, such as the legs and their associated muscles and tendons. He proposes that these changes of form are controlled by morphogenetic fields, but says:

> Although the fields controlling the changes of form of specialized motor structures of animals are in fact morphogenetic fields, they bring about

movements rather than net changes of form. For this reason, it seems preferable to refer to them as motor fields.[18]

This leads to the suggestion of a great variety of motor fields. There are low-level fields that control movements of which we are not normally conscious, such as breathing and the beating of the heart. Then there are higher-level fields, such as those involved in eating and walking, which result from essentially repetitive actions. High-level fields co-ordinate such lower-level fields to produce complex actions such as searching for food, courting and reproduction.

At this point 'movement' develops into what we usually call 'behaviour'. An animal's past movements will, by morphic resonance, influence later movements of a similar type. This will result in more or less fixed patterns of action, or habits. Morphic resonance also provides a means whereby such habits can be transferred from one member of a species to others, so providing an explanation for 'instincts', apparently inborn patterns of behaviour.[19]

Of course there are occasions when an animal has to respond to a new experience. This may result in a new form of activity. It may then be said that the animal has 'learned' something. A new motor field has come into being. This field is now available to other individuals and may, by morphic resonance, facilitate their response to the same experience. In other words, learning to cope with it will be easier for them.[20] This provides the basis for many of the experiments proposed as ways of testing the theory of the existence of morphogenetic fields and morphic resonance.

Evolution

The idea of morphic resonance leads Sheldrake to reject the classical neo-Darwinian interpretation of evolution and to favour a form of neo-Lamarckianism. Thus he says:

The influence of previous organisms on subsequent similar organisms by morphic resonance could give rise to effects which could not conceivably occur if heredity depended only on the transfer of genes and other material structures from parents to their progeny. This possibility enables the question of the 'inheritance of acquired characteristics' to be seen in a new light.[21]

He give as an example the callosities on the knees of camels.

It is easy to understand how these are acquired in response to abrasion of the skin as the camels kneel down. But baby camels are born with them. Facts of this type would make good sense if acquired characteristics somehow became hereditary.[22]

He thinks that this is a more credible explanation than the neo-Darwinian one that the callosities are the result of a random mutation producing an effect that was favoured by natural selection.[23]

A scientific theory?

On one level, the debate about Sheldrake's ideas has been about whether or not what he has proposed can legitimately be called 'scientific'. Lewis Wolpert, a professor of biology, raised this point in an article in *The Guardian*:

For a new theory to be taken seriously, it must at the very least deal with current experimental data as well as current theories. Morphic resonance is totally hopeless in this respect since it does not even touch the data. It merely asserts the action of unmeasurable, non-quantifiable forces. But, cry its defenders, the theory is testable and therefore conforms to Popper's criterion for science. This view completely misunderstands the nature of science. It is possible to hold absurd theories which are testable, but that does not make them science. Consider the hypothesis that the poetic muse resides in tiny particles contained in meat. This could be tested by seeing if eating more hamburgers improved one's poetry.[24]

Wolpert makes a valid point here. Testability may be a necessary criterion of what is 'science', but it is not a sufficient one in practice. The decision by working scientists as to whether a new idea is or is not worth exploring by scientific investigation is sometimes not easy, and is based on quite subtle considerations. In the quotation given, Wolpert refers to one consideration, namely the relationship between the new idea and the existing data. Here at least two points are relevant. First, does the new idea seem likely to provide a more satisfactory explanation of the data than existing ideas? In this case Wolpert, and many others, think not, because it introduces 'unmeasurable and non-quantifiable forces'. Secondly, is the new idea necessary? Sheldrake thinks it is, because he became convinced that the current 'mechanistic' view of biology cannot conceivably provide answers to the outstanding problems in morphogenesis. Most of his fellow-biologists seem to disagree with him and share Wolpert's view that

> We do not have a complete understanding of how hydra regenerates its head when it is removed . . . but there is a wealth of experimental detail and, more important, there are models which provide a very good account of the process of regeneration. They show unequivocally how a physico-chemical system could provide the basis for regeneration of pattern. [25]

John Maddox raised a related, but not quite identical, point in a radio discussion with Sheldrake:

> The conventional scientific view, which I think is entirely proper, is that there is no particular point in inventing theories which in themselves constitute an assault on what we know about the physical world as it stands, when there is at least a chance, and in this case a good chance, in my opinion, that conventional theories will in due course provide an explanation.[26]

There are, of course, examples in the history of science of seemingly 'wild' ideas that challenged current 'common-sense' ideas and that eventually became accepted. This has happened when the evidence in favour of the idea has become too strong to be ignored. What of the evidence for morphogenetic fields and morphic resonance?

The question of evidence

Most of the tests of Sheldrake's ideas that have been made public have been based on the idea of learning assisted by morphic resonance. One of the most public tests was carried out with the help of the BBC television programme *Tomorrow's World* in November 1984. It involved two pictures containing hidden images. These were sent to experimenters all over the world, who tested groups of people to find out what proportion correctly recognized the hidden images within thirty seconds of being shown them. The tests were carried out over a five-day period before the television programme, and then on different people over a five-day period after the programme. On the programme, eight million viewers were shown one of the pictures and the hidden image revealed. After they had learned to recognize it, they were shown the hidden image again. The purpose of the experiment was to see if this made it easier for other people, who had not seen the programme, to spot the hidden image.

The tests were carried out in 121 locations and involved 6,265 people. The results were inconclusive. In Europe there was a statistically significant positive increase in ease of recognition of the hidden image after the programme. In Australia, New Zealand and South Africa there was a small, but statistically non-significant, positive increase. In North America (Canada and the USA) there was no significant effect at all.

After over ten years of experimentation no-one has yet produced evidence that has impressed the sceptics. Even those sympathetic to Sheldrake have to admit that the matter is, at best, still wide open. Colin Tudge, a science journalist who has been publicly supportive since 1981, summed up the situation in 1994 by saying:

> In 1982 *New Scientist* launched a competition with a prize of £250 for the best experimental design to test Sheldrake's ideas. Experiments have been going on around the world ever since. Results have been mixed: some are promising, some not.[27]

He goes on to say that the odds against Sheldrake's ideas being true are probably long.

On the BBC2 programme *Heretic*,[28] some of the academics who have given Sheldrake support over the years expressed the view that now, faced with several experiments that had failed to support his theory, he seemed to be indulging in special pleading to explain these failures when he ought to be doubting the validity of the theory. It is arguable that there is some special pleading in his original book. One example is his refusal to accept that Jewish circumcision invalidates his theory of the inheritance of acquired characteristics. How does it differ in essence from the callosities on the knees of camels? His argument[29] that the callosities developed in a regenerating structure (the skin over the knee) and so altered the pathway of morphogenesis, whereas circumcision is carried out on a fully formed, non-regenerating structure, does seem like an argument that explains away the evidence rather than faces it. In fact, most evolutionary biologists would argue that numerous experiments have failed to provide any clear evidence of the inheritance of acquired characteristics.

Sheldrake has certainly not given up hope of validating his ideas experimentally. His most recent book[30] suggests experiments which the readers might carry out to test his theory for themselves.

The metaphysical implications

One gets the impression that some of the opposition to Sheldrake's ideas has a basis in the critic's metaphysical commitment to a materialistic philosophy. In the final chapter of his first book, Sheldrake seems to attempt to disarm such opposition. He quite rightly says:

> At present, scientific and metaphysical questions are frequently confused with each other, because of the close connection between the mechanistic theory of life and the metaphysical theory of materialism.[31]

He goes on to say that the metaphysical stance would still be defensible even if the mechanistic theory of life were abandoned, though 'it would lose its privileged position; it would have to enter into free competition with other metaphysical theories'. Then he outlines briefly four metaphysical theories in order to show that all four are equally compatible with the hypothesis of formative causation.[32]

The first is what he calls 'modified materialism'. He points out that the concept of 'matter' has changed with advances in science. It now embraces 'energy'. Morphogenetic fields are intimately associated with material systems and so could be regarded as 'aspects of matter'. Such a modified materialism could perhaps embrace, rather than simply deny, some parapsychological phenomena by explaining them in terms of the effects of morphic resonance. It would not, however, be radically different from current metaphysical materialism.

Secondly, there is the dualistic philosophy which accepts the reality of the conscious self as something distinct from the material body which interacts with it. The problem with this view has been the means by which the two interact. Sheldrake suggests that the conscious self could be thought of as interacting with the motor fields, as 'entering into' the fields while remaining over and above them. The conscious self might influence the body through the motor fields either by selecting between different possible fields, so causing one course of action to be adopted rather than another, or it might serve as a creative agency which brings new motor fields into existence. This introduces the factor of 'conscious causation' alongside 'formative causation' and 'energetic causation'. Where does the creativity of the conscious self come from? Is it just a given, the result of chance? Or is it to be attributed to a non-physical creative agency which transcends individual organisms? The second possibility is the basis of the third and fourth metaphysical theories.

The third theory sees the creative force as transcending individual organisms but not all nature. It is immanent within the universe as a whole. This explains evolutionary creativity within the universe, but does not explain the existence of the universe itself. In Sheldrake's view, this leaves the universe without a purpose simply 'evolving continuously, but blindly and without direction'.[33]

Fourthly, there might be a transcendent consciousness which created the universe. This consciousness is not developing towards a goal, but is its own goal. It provides the universe with its cause and purpose.

Sheldrake and Christianity

One gets the impression that the fourth view is the one that Sheldrake espouses. This is confirmed in his later book *The Rebirth of Nature*.[34] This is an avowedly religious book, as indicated by its subtitle *The Greening of Science and God*. In it he provides a glimpse of his own spiritual pilgrimage. He says that at one time he rejected Christianity and explored instead the religious traditions of the East.[35] There is the implication that the reason for this was a sense that Christianity had lost contact with 'mystical insight, with visionary experience, with a sense of life in nature, and with the power of ritual'. This interest in Eastern religions was the reason for going to work in India. To his surprise, however, he found himself drawn back to Christianity, but a form of Christianity in which the power of pilgrimage, of ritual, of seasonal festivals, of meditation and of prayer is a reality.

This is not the place, nor do I have the expertise, to enter into a critique of Sheldrake's rather idiosyncratic and questionable presentation of the history of religion, Christian church history, and the history of science. The important aspects of his book for us are what it shows of his understanding of religious experience and his concept of God.

The link with his earlier books is the theory of formative causation and morphic resonance. He uses this to explain the power of religious rituals and the sense of the sacredness of places. The repeated performance of a ritual creates a morphic field, into which subsequent performers of the ritual tap through morphic resonance. As a result,

> Through morphic resonance, ritual really can bring the past into the present. The present performers of the ritual do indeed connect with those in the past. The greater the similarity between the way it was performed before, the stronger the resonant connection between the past and present participants.[36]

The sense of the 'spirit' of a place he attributes to a morphic field that has developed as a result of patterns of activity that have happened there, so that 'particular places will have their own memories by self-resonance with their own past'.[37] To some extent this is brought to the place by people, whose memory of their previous experience in the place, or in similar places, will tend to affect their present experience. But there is, he suggests, through morphic resonance, 'a component of collective memory, through which people can tune into the past experiences of other people in the same place'.[38] Through morphic resonance, however, one place can participate in the morphic field of another, similar place.

Before gladly embracing all this as a vindication of spiritual and mystical experiences related to holy places, one ought to stop and consider whether or not this theory does not undermine such experiences, by attributing them to a more or less automatic, mechanistic process (even it it is non-material and non-energetic!). There is no room here for experiencing a graciously given encounter with a divine person. Instead there is participation in a force field which people can generate for themselves by the correct performance of a ritual. The more mechanical that performance the better, because the more exact the repetition, the more quickly it builds up a morphic field.

Sheldrake's concept of God is expounded in the chapter on 'The Greening of God'. It seems clear that he is concerned to present God as embracing all polarities, especially femininity and masculinity, and so being the ground of unity for the cosmos, and also as intimately involved in the history of the world and of humanity. It is significant that he appeals to the experience of mystics of both the East and the West, to the claims of James Frazer about the animistic and shamanistic roots of Judaism and Christianity, to popular veneration of the Virgin Mary, and to the theory of evolution, but hardly at all to the Bible. This is very much an experience-based theology. The result is an acceptance of what he calls 'the new evolutionary view of God', which he expresses by quoting from two process theologians:

> God is not the world and the world is not God. But God includes the world. God perfects the world and the world perfects God. There is no world apart

from God, and there is no God apart from some world. Of course there are differences. Whereas no world can exist without God, God can exist without *this* world . . . since God, like all living things, only perfectly, embodies the principle of internal relations, God's life depends on there being some world to include.[39]

This is what has come to be known as *panentheism* ('all is in God'). Unlike classical pantheism ('all is God'), it does not equate God with the universe. As in classical theism, God is seen as transcending the universe. However, God is no longer regarded as existing independently. God's freedom, it is argued, is preserved because of not being dependent on any *particular* universe, but God cannot exist apart from *some* universe. Moreover, God is so intimately involved with that universe that he learns and grows as a result of the experiences that follow from this involvement.

One of the attractions of a panentheistic concept of God is that it seems to solve one of the major problems of classical theism, namely its impassive image of God, an image that seems at odds with the biblical picture of a loving God who is involved with the world and people. It is arguably, however, a solution which creates problems as great as those it tries to solve. For example, how can a God who grows and learns be eternally perfect? Is a God who is not eternally perfect a being who deserves our total confidence and commitment? And how does all this relate to the God revealed in the Bible? We will discuss panentheism further later on (see pages 153–156).

Sheldrake and New Age ideas

The attraction of Sheldrake's ideas for adherents of the New Age movement should now be fairly obvious. Like Capra, he has the authority of a scientist (still, it seems, important for some New Agers, and very helpful in dialogue with conventional people) and yet shares their critique of the materialistic, mechanistic, reductionist cast of the thinking of most scientists.

The theory of formative causation and its concept of morphic fields and morphic resonance can be transmuted to fit in with ideas about the mystical auras associated with living beings and the vibrations emanating from, or concentrated by, crystals. It also gives an under-girding to New Agers' interest in, and apparent enjoyment of, rituals of various kinds. It offers an explanation of the significance of sacred sites.

Very important, too, is Sheldrake's espousal of panentheism and the 'green' view of God which he bases on it. This leads naturally to our next major topic, ecology and the New Age movement.

9

THE GAIA HYPOTHESIS

In the early 1960s, James Lovelock was a consultant to the team in NASA which was devising ways and means of detecting life on Mars and other planets. Lovelock's speciality was in the design of scientific instruments, but involvement in the project prompted him to think about the basic problem of detecting the presence of life. He concluded that one of the most general characteristics of living organisms is that they are able to take energy from their environment (in the form of sunlight or food) and use it to bring about chemical reactions which would not otherwise occur. As a result, inside living organisms there exists an unusual state of chemical disequilibrium. This is expressed in technical scientific language by saying that within living organisms there is a state of reduced entropy. Lovelock went on to argue:

> Assuming that life on any planet would be bound to use the fluid media – oceans, atmosphere, or both – as conveyor-belts for raw materials and waste products, it occurred to me that some of the activity associated with concentrated entropy reduction within a living system might spill over into the conveyor-belt regions and alter their composition. The atmosphere of a life-bearing planet would thus become recognizably different from that of a dead planet.[1]

He therefore examined the chemical composition of the atmosphere of the Earth and its two neighbouring planets, Mars and Venus. The composition of the atmospheres of Mars and Venus could be determined quite readily using the well-established technique of infrared spectroscopy.

The results of this study were striking, as can be seen in the table below.[2] The Earth's atmosphere is markedly different from that of the other two planets, despite the fact that in composition and size they are quite similar to the Earth. The reason for the difference is that the atmospheres on Venus and Mars are what one would expect for systems at chemical equilibrium, given their size and the amounts of energy they receive from the Sun. The Earth's atmosphere is a long way from chemical equilibrium. Oxygen, for example, is highly reactive chemically, and readily combines with various substances on the Earth's surface (as in the rusting of iron). One would therefore expect there to be only traces of it free in the atmosphere, as on the other planets. If the Earth's atmosphere were at chemical equilibrium it would be very similar to that of Venus with regard to the amounts of the gases listed. Something must be keeping the Earth's atmosphere in its state of disequilibrium. Lovelock argues that it is the presence of living organisms.

Gas	Venus	Earth	Mars
Carbon dioxide	98%	0.03%	95%
Nitrogen	1.9%	79%	2.7%
Oxygen	trace	21%	0.13%
Argon	0.1%	1%	2%

The sea is also in a state of chemical disequilibrium. Given the overall composition of the Earth's crust, which is constantly being eroded and washed into the sea, and the composition of the atmosphere, it is possible to estimate the expected amount of salt in the sea.[3] It ought to be 13%. In fact it is 3.5%. Once again Lovelock attributes this to the presence of life on Earth.

It has been known for quite some time that there are 'cycles' in nature which operate to maintain an environmental *status quo*. For example, air-breathing animals take in oxygen and breathe out carbon dioxide.

Plants, however, are able to take up the carbon dioxide and return oxygen into the air. As a result, other things being equal (which they are not at present!), there is a balance struck which maintains the amount of carbon dioxide in the atmosphere at a more or less constant level. Moreover, following Darwin, it has been generally accepted that the environment has a profound effect on living organisms. They must adapt to their environment. Those which adapt most successfully are likely to persist. What Lovelock did was to argue that the converse of this is also true: organisms profoundly influence their environment in such a way as to produce and maintain that environment as close to the optimum for the continuance of life as possible. This does not simply affect its immediate locality, because the sea and the air are ultimately the common environment of all life forms on Earth. Lovelock's colleague, Lynn Margulis, puts it as follows:

> Each species to a greater or lesser degree modifies its environment to optimize its reproduction rate. Gaia follows from this by being the sum total of all these individual modifications and by the fact that all species are connected, for the production of gases, food and waste removal, however circuitously, to all others.[4]

By 'Gaia', Lovelock and Margulis mean the whole global ecosystem, regarded as a single complex entity 'involving the Earth's biosphere, atmosphere, oceans, and soil'.[5] Acceptance of this way of looking at the planet does produce quite a change in perspective. The conventional view tends to see the living organisms on the Earth as largely passive, simply responding to changes in their environment which are brought about by geophysical processes that go on heedless of them. The Gaia hypothesis gives the living organisms an active role in shaping the planet so that it is congenial for life.

Lovelock makes use of ideas from cybernetics to develop the concept of Gaia. Cybernetics is the science which is concerned with self-regulating systems of communication and control in both machines and living organisms. An important element in self-regulating control systems are 'feedback loops'. The thermostat on a central-heating system is perhaps one of the most familiar examples. As the temperature in a room falls the thermostat senses this, and when it falls below a set level it switches on the power to the heater. It also senses the rising temperature and switches the heating off when it goes above the set maximum level. This is a typical 'negative feedback loop', and such loops are an effective way of maintaining a system in a fairly stable state because they oppose changes in the system (in the temperature in this case). This example illustrates an important feature of control systems. Only a small amount of power is needed to operate the thermostat, but it can control a heating system which uses a vastly greater amount of power. The difference in the amounts of power is the 'gain' or amplification achieved by the control system.

The Earth is covered with a multitude of ecosystems. These do not have clearly defined boundaries, but overlap and interact. This is even true of ecosystems separated by thousands of miles. Deforestation in the Himalayas has changed the ecosystem on their slopes. As a result, monsoon rains run off more quickly than they used to, leading to flooding in the low-lying coastal areas of Bangladesh, so affecting the ecosystem there. Each ecosystem has its own self-regulating feedback systems. Together the systems form an interacting network of systems in which another level of feedback systems operates, and so on. At least, that is what Lovelock hypothesizes:

> We have . . . defined Gaia as a complex entity involving the Earth's biosphere, atmosphere, oceans, and soil: the totality constituting a feedback or cybernetic system which seeks an optimal physical and chemical environment for life on this planet. The maintenance of relatively constant conditions by active control may be conveniently described by the term 'homoeostasis'.[6]

The Gaia hypothesis has stirred up a good deal of controversy among scientists, and we will consider some of the major areas of debate.

Is it testable?

For a theory to have scientific credibility it needs to be testable. This is normally done by using the theory to make predictions which can be tested by experiment or observation. In a paper in *Nature*[7] Lovelock cites some testable predictions derived from the Gaia hypothesis. These include the following.

1. The prediction, made in 1968, that there is no life on Mars. The Viking mission in 1977 failed to find any evidence of life on the planet.

2. In 1971 Lovelock predicted that there must be a mechanism whereby living organisms promote the transfer of essential elements from the oceans to the land. In 1973 he established that marine algae convert sulphate ions in sea water into the volatile gas dimethyl sulphide. These algae also produce methyl iodide. In this way sulphur and iodine, both essential for maintaining life on land, are returned to the land from which they have been removed by the erosion of minerals.

3. In 1981 he predicted that there is a biological mechanism for regulating the amount of carbon dioxide in the atmosphere by enhancing the weathering of rocks. This was confirmed in 1989 when it was found that micro-organisms have an effect on rock weathering.

The evidence, however, is not all in Lovelock's favour. He has argued that the dimethyl sulphide produced by algal plankton in the deep oceans has an effect on the cloud cover. This is because under the influence of sunlight the dimethyl sulphide is converted into acids, tiny droplets of which form the nuclei around which vapour condenses to produce clouds. Since clouds reflect the light and heat of the Sun back into space, their formation leads to a cooling of the Earth's surface under them. This, presumably, would mean that the plankton would grow less rapidly, and so the production of dimethyl sulphide would fall. Here would be another negative feedback mechanism, stabilizing the temperature. On the basis of this argument one might expect that the production of dimethyl sulphide would have increased at the end of the last Ice Age as the surface temperature of the Earth increased. However, evidence from Antarctic ice cores shows the opposite to have been the case. Faced with this evidence, Lovelock has proposed a couple of reasons[8] why the Ice Age might have led to increased production of dimethyl sulphide by marine algae: the locking up of water in the ice caps would have made the sea saltier, and this may have led to greater production of the gas by algae; and glaciers may have been more effective than rivers in moving biomass into the seas, so increasing the amount of nutrient available for algal growth.

Lovelock's response to the ice-core evidence illustrates why some argue that the Gaia hypothesis is not really scientific. Taking their stand on the ideas of the philosopher Karl Popper,[9] they argue that a scientific theory must not only produce testable predictions, but, more importantly, it must be falsifiable. The problem with the Gaia hypothesis is that it involves so many complexities that, when faced with apparently contradictory data, it is nearly always possible to think up some way of explaining these away. Kirchner has argued, for this kind of reason, that the hypothesis is inherently unfalsifiable.[10]

Many scientists and philosophers of science regard the falsifiability criterion as too restrictive as a requirement for a theory to be 'scientific'. Scientific theories can be of many different kinds, with differing degrees of rigour. Colin Russell uses Mary Hesse's classification of scientific statements[11] in a discussion of the Gaia hypothesis and concludes that 'the Gaia hypothesis may be properly described at present as scientific theory, *but only in the form of a "conceptual model"*.'[12]

Is it metaphysical?

Some scientists, such as W. Ford Doolittle[13] and Richard Dawkins,[14] have claimed that the Gaia hypothesis is unscientific because it requires the existence of a purposive force or agent, over and above the 'blind' forces of nature, to ensure a planet-wide co-operation and control of living organisms.

They argue that, assuming that evolution proceeds by natural selection at the local level, there is no reason to expect the evolution of a planet-wide altruistic behaviour with organisms all over the world co-operating for their mutual benefit to produce the optimum conditions for life. In fact an organism which 'cheated' by putting no effort into the planet-wide effort but let others do all the work would be at an advantage. It would have more energy to put into its own survival and so would leave more offspring. Unless there were some central control to force individuals to exercise constraint, therefore, the whole system would soon break down as organisms that 'cheated' became dominant.

Lovelock has responded to this criticism by producing a computerized model called 'Daisyworld'.[15] This is a planet like the Earth, but the only life forms on it are two species of daisies, one white and the other black. These daisies grow best at a temperature of 20°C and will die if the temperature rises above 40°C or falls below 5°C. The average temperature of the planet depends on the balance between the heat received from its sun and the heat radiated back into space. The daisies can influence this. The white daisies reflect away radiation from the sun and so cool the planet. The black daisies absorb the radiation and so warm the planet. As it ages, Daisysun, like our Sun, becomes brighter, so that Daisyworld receives more heat from it.

What the computer program shows is that, for a long period in the existence of the Daisyworld-Daisysun system, life in the form of the daisies can survive on Daisyworld despite the rising heat output of Daisysun. This is because, when the heat output is low and most of the white daisies die of cold, the black daisies are good at absorbing the heat and so warming the planet. As Daisysun gets hotter, the black daisies wilt and die with the heat, but the white ones reflect Daisysun's radiation away, so keeping themselves cool and cooling the planet. Of course a time comes when even they cannot keep the planetary temperature below 40°C and all the daisies die, leaving a sterile planet. However, here is a simple negative feedback system which keeps the conditions close to the optimum for life for a considerable period simply through the operation of a form of natural selection. No metaphysical purposive force is needed. The model can be made more complex by adding more species of daisies (including grey daisies that 'cheat' by not helping to regulate the temperature), plagues which kill off large numbers of the daisies, herbivores which eat them, and carnivores which eat the herbivores. The negative feedback system still operates.

This model system, Lovelock argues, shows that regulatory behaviour such as he postulates for Gaia can develop simply as a property of the complex processes which link organisms to their environment. The Gaia hypothesis, he insists, says that global homoeostasis 'is maintained by active feedback systems which operate automatically and unconsciously'.[16] Daisyworld does demonstrate that this is a possibility. It does not prove that this is in fact the case on Earth.

On the basis of the behaviour of the Daisyworld model in response to sudden perturbations (such as an asteroid impact or a plague killing most of the daisies), Lovelock expresses a strong preference for the 'punctuated equilibrium' interpretation of evolution put forward by Stephen Gould and Niles Eldredge.[17] This has made the Gaia hypothesis unpopular with the opponents of 'punctuated equilibrium', such as Richard Dawkins.

Is Gaia alive?

According to Lovelock, 'The Gaia hypothesis supposes the Earth to be alive, and considers what evidence there is for and against the supposition.'[18] When he says that the Earth is alive, he does not mean simply that there are living creatures on it. He means that all these living creatures are best regarded as forming a single living organism, Gaia. As a result, he says,

> Gaia as the largest manifestation of life differs from other living organisms of Earth in the way that you or I differ from our living population of cells.[19]

He is also prepared to say that, in a limited sense, Gaia is intelligent:

> Indeed, all cybernetic systems are intelligent to the extent that they must give the correct answer to at least one question. If Gaia exists, then she is without doubt intelligent in this limited sense.[20]

Because he regards Gaia as a living organism, Lovelock says that it is no longer helpful to talk about 'geophysics'. Instead we should talk and think about 'geophysiology'. Writing of his reaction to the criticisms of his first book about Gaia, he says that he was

> . . . led to new and deeper insights into Gaia. In a physiological sense the Earth was alive . . . this second book is a statement of Gaia theory; the basis

of a new and unified view of the Earth and life sciences. Because Gaia was seen from outside as a physiological system, I have called the science of Gaia geophysiology.[21]

This claim that the Earth, under the guise of Gaia, should be thought of as a living organism has created a good deal of controversy, for two main reasons.

The first reason concerns Lovelock's definition of life. He complains that while 'we all know intuitively what life is . . . scientists, who are notorious for their indecent curiosity, shy away from defining life'.[22] He cites the fact that there is no definition of life in a standard dictionary of biology. He finds the definitions in *Webster's Dictionary* and *The Oxford English Dictionary* 'manifestly inadequate'.[23]

In an extended discussion, Lovelock settles on three characteristics[24] which he takes as defining a life: it is social; it has the property of homoeostasis; and it protects itself by a boundary. Gaia, he asserts, has all these three properties. It is made up of all the live forms on the planet; it regulates the environment by negative feedback mechanisms to ensure that it is the optimum for the continuation of life; and the atmosphere forms a protective boundary. One problem with this definition is his stress on the social aspect of life. Realizing that it is problematic, he appeals to the fact that we recognize nations and tribes as distinct entities. This is fair enough, but I doubt whether most people would be willing to accept that nations are living creatures! For conventional biologists the major weakness in Lovelock's definition is that it is too restricted. Certainly all living organisms have boundaries, operate a measure of homoeostatic control within them, and interact with their environment, but they show other essential characteristics too (growth and reproduction being important ones). Lovelock's criteria are necessary, but not sufficient, for regarding an entity as 'living'.

Significantly, even Lynn Margulis, a co-creator of the Gaia hypothesis, is not happy with talk of Gaia as a living organism:

I reject Jim's statement 'The Earth is alive'; this metaphor, stated this way, alienates precisely those scientists who should be working in a Gaian context. I do not agree with the formulation that says 'Gaia is an organism'. First of all in this context no-one has defined 'organism'. Furthermore I do not think that Gaia is a singularity. Rather Gaia is an extremely complex system with identifiable regulatory properties which are very specific to the lower atmosphere.[25]

The debate about the Gaia hypothesis has been fruitful at least in the sense that, by producing a new perspective on old problems, it has made scientists in fields like geophysics and atmospheric chemistry take more seriously the possible role of living organisms. If Lovelock had restricted the hypothesis to the claim that there exists a network of planet-wide, non-living environmental control systems which involve both biotic and abiotic mechanisms, he would probably have had a much more sympathetic reception and achieved much the same results in terms of scientific understanding of global ecology.

The second reason the claim that the Earth is alive has aroused controversy is that it opens the door to animistic ideas about 'Mother Earth' which are inimical to science. Lovelock tries to disclaim responsibility for the more extreme developments in this direction, commenting that 'Gaia is an empty sign . . . filling fast, and mostly with rubbish, like an empty skip left on a London street'.[26] However, the danger was there when he accepted the suggestion of his friend William Golding, the well-known novelist, to give his hypothesis the name the Greeks used for the Earth goddess, the consort of Uranus, the sky god. If the connotations were lost on Lovelock, they certainly were not on other people. He comments, with surprise, that two thirds of the letters he received after his first book were about the meaning of Gaia in a religious context.[27]

Colin Russell has pointed out the dangers of a return to an 'organismic' view of the Earth, such as that which predominated in Europe up to the seventeenth century.[28] It was uncongenial to science as we know it, and the rise of modern science was due to the demythologizing of nature and the replacement of this view by a more mechanistic one. This was helped, at least in part, by the revival of a biblical theology of nature as the creation of a sovereign God who impressed laws on inanimate matter. Russell argues that, in what he calls the 'Strong Form' that 'the Earth is alive', the Gaia hypothesis goes beyond legitimate (and useful) metaphor and reverts to myth.[29] He points out that in this form it has some striking similarities to Western alchemy, and that in some kinds of New Age thought there have been attempts to revive at one and the same time both alchemical and Gaian mysticism. This attempt to return to a pre-scientific era, Russell asserts, presents us with two stark alternatives:

> Let nature take care of itself and Gaia be free to undergo self-regulation in her own way; or let us draw on the immense bank of scientific knowledge to find new ways of sustaining life on the planet. The first option, to abandon a scientific world view, is to solve nothing and at the same time to bring untold suffering on fellow-human beings; it is the law of the Victorian *laissez-faire* jungle. Do we really want infant mortality, mass hunger and epidemic diseases at the 17th century rates? We don't even have a 17th century population. The second option has many risks but surely they are worth taking. How else can we feed the hungry, heal the sick, sustain in a degree of wellbeing the masses who will populate our vast cities?[30]

God and Gaia

Although Lovelock was surprised when so many people read religious connotations into the Gaia hypothesis, he was not displeased. He makes his own religious position clear:

> For the present, my belief in God rests at the stage of positive agnosticism. I am too deeply committed to science for undiluted faith; equally unacceptable to me spiritually is the materialist world of undiluted fact. Art and science seem inter-connected with each other and with religion, and to be mutually enlarging. That Gaia can be both spiritual and scientific is, for me, deeply satisfying.[31]

In so far as Lovelock derives religious ideas from his hypothesis, he seems to move in the direction of a pantheistic Mother Goddess. It is significant that in his discussion of 'God and Gaia' he has much more sympathy for the veneration of the Virgin Mary than for the concept of God that he attributes to the Judaeo-Christian tradition, a God who is 'remote, all-powerful, all-seeing'.[32] Such a God, he says, is 'either frightening or unapproachable'. This is a caricature of the God presented in the Bible, who is certainly all-powerful, all-seeing and awe-inspiring, but is certainly not remote or unapproachable. Mary, he says, is 'close and manageable' (a classic expression of the human tendency to 'make God in our own image' in order to be able to manipulate him/her?). He goes on to speculate:

> What if Mary is another name for Gaia? Then her capacity for virgin birth is no miracle or parthenogenetic aberration, it is a role of Gaia since life began. Immortals do not need to reproduce images of themselves; it is enough to renew continuously the life that constitutes them. Any living organism a quarter as old as the Universe itself and still full of vigour is as near immortal as we ever need to know. She is of this Universe and, conceivably, a part of God. On Earth she is the source of life everlasting and is alive now; she gave birth to humankind and we are part of her.[33]

Here is an amazing piece of mythologizing of the figure of the Mary, the peasant woman who was the mother of Jesus of Nazareth, which totally ignores the historical people and events at the heart of the Christian good news, which, we shall argue later, provides a far sounder basis for an ecological approach to life than this woolly mythology. There is the implication, at least, that the universe is God in a pantheistic sense. The Earth then is also divine, but so are you and I. Later on he seems to imply that 'the intuition of God' may be a suitable 'metaphor of a living Universe'.[34]

It is important to recognize that here Lovelock is blurring the boundary between Gaia as a *scientific hypothesis* and Gaia as a *myth*. The move from the one to other is not necessary, and it does not help acceptance of the hypothesis as serious science. Moreover, even if the scientific hypothesis were well established, it would not entail the truth of the mythological concept of Gaia. It would establish that there are planet-wide automatic and unconscious feedback *mechanisms*, not that the Earth is a living *organism*, let alone a goddess.

10

ECOLOGY AND NEW AGE SPIRITUALITY

> What people do about their ecology depends on what they think about themselves in relation to things around them. Human ecology is deeply conditioned by beliefs about our nature and destiny – that is, by religion.[1]

So said Professor Lynn White in a very influential article entitled 'The Historic Roots of Our Ecologic Crisis'.

Evidence that he was right is to be seen in the fact that the growing ecological concern of the last two decades has produced a number of different forms of 'spirituality', both inside and outside the traditional religions. 'Spirituality' is one of those slippery words that is difficult to define because it is used differently by different people. I am using it in the sense of 'a response to life which takes seriously a non-material dimension of reality which transcends the individual consciousness'. This rise in 'green spirituality' has been a marked feature of the New Age movement.

New Age green spirituality

As was indicated in our brief opening survey of the New Age movement, the interest in, and concern for, green issues held by many

131

New Agers follows naturally from their monistic and pantheistic outlook.

If 'all is one', we are intimately related to the rest of the cosmos in general, and of planet Earth in particular. Ecology shows us something of this inter-relatedness, because it is the science which studies how living organisms relate to one another and to their environment. A true monist will be concerned to recognize this oneness with the rest of planet Earth and live in the light of it. Preserving the balance and integrity of nature, which is an expression of the unity of all things, will be a prime concern.

Pantheism heightens this concern about ecology and the environment. If 'all is God', then the other entities on planet Earth are also innately divine and deserve not just my respect but my worship. I shall want to avoid doing them any harm. An extreme expression of this is seen in Jainism, a pantheistic Indian religion. When walking, the devout Jain wears a covering over the mouth and nose, to avoid breathing in any insects and so killing them, and sweeps the ground ahead to remove any insects which otherwise might be trodden on and killed.

But how does this work out in practice for New Agers? It seems to me that there are three main types of New Age green spirituality.

The mystical approach

This is based on monism and may rest on a monistic mystical experience, such as that described by Kit Pedler (co-creator of the very successful TV series *Doomwatch*):

> On one occasion I was looking at a ripening field of barley and was concluding on a rather intellectual level, 'what a beautiful colour' – without any real involvement in the thought. Then I went on to think over the views I have tried to express here, and then without warning, my mind shut off and everything went quiet and I began to be aware in an entirely different way. The gradations of colour and the waves of the wind undulating through the hairs of the grain became a nearly unbearably intense experience: a feeling of beauty which I have never before known. Every sense intensified to a level where I cried out in delight. The colours became a whole event complete and unanalysable: they were touchable, I could smell

them and feel them, they were all shades of gold and brown. Their intensity almost burnt my eyes. I was the grain, I was the colours. I have no way of knowing, in clock time, how long this experience lasted, but it ceased just as suddenly as it began and gradually my ordinary brain began to think again.[2]

Fritjof Capra describes a somewhat similar experience:

I was sitting by the ocean one late summer afternoon, watching the waves rolling in and feeling the rhythm of my breathing, when I suddenly became aware of my whole environment as being engaged in a gigantic cosmic dance. Being a physicist, I knew that the sand, rocks, water and air around me were made up of vibrating molecules and atoms, and that these consisted of particles which interacted with one another by creating and destroying other particles. I knew also that the Earth's atmosphere was continually bombarded by showers of 'cosmic rays', particles of high energy undergoing multiple collisions as they penetrated the air. All this was familiar to me from my research in high-energy physics, but until that moment I had only experienced it through graphs, diagrams and mathematical theories. As I sat on that beach my former experiences came to life; I 'saw' cascades of energy coming down from outer space, in which particles were created and destroyed in rhythmic pulses; I 'saw' the atoms of the elements and those of my body participating in this cosmic dance of energy; I felt its rhythm and I 'heard' its sound, and at that moment I *knew* that this was the Dance of Shiva, the Lord of Dancers worshipped by the Hindus.[3]

In an earlier chapter (pages 60–63), we have suggested how such experiences can be understood within a trinitarian Christian framework. Because of their prior philosophical commitments, both Pedler and Capra interpreted their experiences in a monistic way.

Monism leads to a stress on the inter-connectedness, inter-dependence and equal value of all things. This gives rise to concerns such as preservation of the integrity of ecosystems, the sustainable use of non-renewable resources, and justice in the sharing of resources. Laudable as these concerns are (and I share them), monism also raises some major questions.

First, what are the status and place of humans on Planet Earth? Logically monism leads to the view that all things have equal status. Some New Agers do indeed deny that there are any 'human rights' distinct from the rights of any other life forms, or indeed inanimate forms, on Earth. In practice, of course, some differences do have to be accepted. Cows eat grass. Humans can become vegetarians but not total abstainers from food and drink. Nevertheless, the tendency in monism is to minimize the difference between humans and other life forms on this planet. Pedler, for example, struggles with this problem:

> But what about the rights of the cabbage? If occupancy and existence are the basis of rights, then vegetables have rights; and if we do not eat meat then we have either to kill vegetables or starve. So we eat living things and offend those rights. Here again we can only compromise and eat the minimum commensurate with health, and thus learn to *tread more lightly upon the earth.*[4]

The problem is that there is no basis in monism for making any qualitative distinction between humans and other forms of life.

A second question arises from the attraction of monism for some environmentalists. This is that, by placing equal value on all things, it might seem to provide a basis for extending the moral values which govern inter-personal relationships to govern our relations with whales and woodlands. In fact, instead of doing this, it calls into question the whole concept of morality. Moral values rest on the claim that certain things 'ought' to be so, even if that is not the way things are now. The 'ought/is' distinction is fundamental to morality. But, if 'all is one', and ultimately right/wrong distinctions are illusory, how can I sustain this distinction? Moreover, if 'all is one', I should not seek to change the way things are for fear of disturbing the existing oneness. Thus for Pedler, as he says in the above quotation, the only basis for 'rights' is 'occupancy and existence', and this applies as much to cabbages as to humans. This is compounded if that oneness is a divine being, as in pantheism. Then to oppose what 'is' means opposing God's will. All this leads to a 'quietist' attitude towards natural calamities and social problems which has in fact been a feature of the Eastern monistic religions. They have not been characterized by the protests of the prophet and the reformer in the way that the theistic religions have been.

The animistic approach

This type of spirituality is based on pantheism. If 'all is God' then I can expect to see God in the animals, trees, rivers and other aspects of nature. Traditionally, many pantheistic religions have expressed this in terms of recognizing and worshipping the 'spirits' of various animals, plants and places. As one modern animist explains:

> My perception of what Totemism/Animism means, in its anthropo-morphised form, is that each member of a class of beings (animal, vegetable or mineral) has a 'spirit being' associated with it, and in addition contributes to a more general 'spirit being' relating to the whole class of beings, and thence on until eventually a single, overall, 'Nature Spirit' is reached encompassing all the lesser forms. Pantheism falls out of this naturally.[5]

This view is called 'animism' because the Latin word for 'spirit' is *animus*. As White said, the advent of Christianity in many cultures has led to the questioning, and often the disappearance, of animism. The resurgence of animistic thinking in the New Age has led to a revival of interest in pre-Christian animistic religions, such as Norse religion, Celtic Druidism, and the religions indigenous to North America before the advent of Europeans and Christianity.

How does all this affect the approach to green issues? It leads to a worship of nature, as Nigel Pennick explains:

> This personification of the Earth, seeing it as a sacred being rather than an enormous inanimate rock, is the fundamental worldview. As an extension of this, all aspects of the natural world should be revered, as should places of power within it: locations where the gods are present. Sacred places in the landscape are recognised by their special qualities as places where, by meditation, prayer, ritual and ceremony, one may gain access to states of enlightenment.[6]

Such a worship results in opposition to any change or development that might be regarded as in any way detrimental to the integrity of nature or the well-being of non-human species. In theory, at least, humans are no more divine than any other aspect of nature, and so have no special claims or rights.

Animism shares the problems of the mystical approach. It raises others also. The members of the Findhorn Community in Scotland, for example, claim that they are in touch with the 'devas', the spirits of nature, and that the way we should live is to work with nature by petitioning the nature spirits. Machaelle Wright claims that when caterpillars attacked her cabbages, she did not use a pesticide but petitioned the devas of the caterpillars, and they obliged her by not devastating the plants.[7] There is a problem here regarding the relative rights of the different elements of nature and their spirits. Did the caterpillars simply go off to someone else's cabbages? What about the rights of *those* cabbages not to be eaten by caterpillars rather than humans? Or were the caterpillars simply altruistic and starved to death? What then of the birds and other creatures that need the caterpillars as their food supply? Above all, what about the HIV virus? All viruses are parasitic on living cells, which they take over and eventually kill in order to reproduce themselves. How is the animist to deal with the HIV virus which, according to this world-view, is as divine as the person infected?

Is petition a substitute for political action? When a factory pollutes the environment, do I petition the devas of the plants and animals affected (or the deva of the factory), or do I take political action to get anti-pollution legislation enacted and enforced?

The animistic approach is often commended on quite fallacious historical grounds. It is quite common to find people echoing White's claim that our environmental problems are the result of the demise of animistic religions, with their reverence of nature, in the face of Christianity.

> By destroying pagan animism, Christianity made it possible to exploit nature in a mood of indifference to the feelings of natural objects.[8]

History does not bear out the environmentally friendly nature of animism. Responding to White's claim, Colin Russell argues:

There is plenty of evidence which, at the very least, goes far in exonerating the Christian Church for our ecologic crisis. Consider, for example, the rape of the forest on the Mediterranean seaboard in the pre-Christian era; the fetid pollution of many rivers in the Indian sub-continent; the endangered species in Buddhist lands; the appalling air-pollution in inner-city Tokyo. In none of these has Christianity been at all involved.[9]

Westerners tend to have a false, romantic idea of how animistic societies regard nature. Animistic religions do allow for the control of nature by cutting down trees and killing animals, for instance, by providing rituals to placate the spirits which might object to such actions. In practice many animistic societies see themselves almost in a state of war with the 'wild', as Dr Jon Kirby has shown with regard to the Anufu of Ghana:

> From time immemorial, fire has been a wall of culture against the 'wild' which has been thought of as inexhaustible, evil, dangerous, unknown and useless for any socialised purpose. It [fire] has been man's primary ally in the constant work of domesticating the 'wild'.[10]

The readiness of animistic societies to control nature has its parallel within the New Age movement, and this leads to the third main approach to green issues.

The occultic approach

Animism readily slides into occultism. The basic difference is the shift from petitioning nature to seeking to control its hidden powers, from worshipping the spirits to seeking to share their powers by one means or another.

The New Age has produced a revival of mediumship ('channelling') and magic (Wicca). Some New Agers are themselves worried about this, both because it gives the New Age movement a bad image and because they recognize that the occult is dangerous ground. You may think that you are gaining control over the spirits or powers of nature, but all too often it ends up with them controlling you. Even some New Agers recognize that there are 'mischievous' spirits. For the Christian who takes the Bible seriously there can be no question of dabbling with the occult. The Bible specifically forbids it.

Wicca takes a variety of forms,[11] but the many different gods and goddesses are seen ultimately as manifestations of one divine force. As Vivianne Crowley puts it:

> Wicca worships the divine in the way of our ancient ancestors which is as the Triple Goddess and a Dual God. These are seen as ultimately two aspects of the one divine force which is beyond male and female.[12]

New Age witchcraft is particularly attractive to some feminists. This is because much of it is centred on reverence for the Earth as the Mother Goddess from whom we spring and who supports us. It is possible to tap into her powers by means of the right rituals. The rituals may be performed simply for the experience of the power and the sense of oneness with the goddess which this brings. Or they may be performed in order to make use of the powers for various ends. There have been examples of covens objecting to development plans because they would affect ritual sites where, they claim, it is particularly easy to get in touch with the powers of Mother Earth.

The Gaia hypothesis

This view cuts across all these three approaches. What began as a purely scientific hypothesis has been taken up and used, or abused, in various ways by New Agers.

As we have seen, there is no doubt that when James Lovelock put forward the Gaia hypothesis, he intended it as a serious scientific proposal that the Earth is a unified, but unconscious and purely mechanistic, self-regulating system. By giving his hypothesis the name of the Greek goddess of the Earth, however, he made it easy for people to give it a religious interpretation which was never originally intended. It should be obvious how the idea of the Earth as a living, unified organism, now apparently validated by science, can be laid under tribute to support the kind of ideas that have just been outlined briefly. The quotation from Pennick about the worship of nature, given above, is an example of how this is being done in a fairly moderate way.

An extreme example of this is Peter Russell's book *The Awakening Earth: The Global Brain.*[13] Russell argues that Gaia is a living, conscious organism and that we humans are now her brain. We could become a malignant growth which Gaia will destroy in the interest of her survival. However, he is sure that this will not be the case. Through enlightenment and a change of consciousness we will evolve to a single planetary consciousness, which he calls the 'gaiafield'. There are, he believes, millions of 'gaias' in the galaxy and he envisages all of the gaiafields linking up through a kind of extrasensory perception to produce a unified galactic consciousness. The next level will be the integration of the consciousness of the super-clusters of galaxies. Eventually the whole universe will become a single conscious being, the 'Brahman' of Hindu belief. The possibility that we live in an oscillating universe is welcomed by Russell. He interprets the successive cycles of expansion and contraction as successive reincarnations of Brahman on the way to ultimate perfection.

We have seen in chapter 9 that as a scientific proposal the Gaia hypothesis has only limited empirical support at present, but it deserves further study. We should, however, recognize the New Age use of the idea for what it is – another example of metaphysical speculation which has no direct support in the existing scientific proposal.

11

GREEN CHRISTIANITY

> Christianity, in absolute contrast to ancient paganism ... not only
> established a dualism of man and nature but also insisted that it is God's
> will that man exploit nature for his proper ends ... we shall continue to
> have a worsening ecologic crisis until we reject the Christian axiom that
> nature has no reason for existence save to serve man.[1]

So writes Lynn White. His article, already quoted in the previous
chapter, set a trend in blaming Christianity for our environmental
problems. In particular this criticism has centred on what has often been
called the 'cultural mandate' in Genesis 1:26–28:

> Then God said, 'Let us make man in our image, after our likeness; and let
> them have dominion over the fish of the sea, and over the birds of the air,
> and over the cattle, and over all the earth, and over every creeping thing
> that creeps upon the earth.' So God created man in his own image, in the
> image of God he created him; male and female he created them. And God
> blessed them, and God said to them, 'Be fruitful and multiply, and fill the
> earth and subdue it; and have dominion over the fish of the sea and over
> the birds of the air and over every living thing that moves upon the
> earth.'

Are the critics right? Is Christianity environmentally harmful? Can
there be a truly Christian basis for environmental concern? In short, can

Christianity be 'green'? There are, in fact, five distinctly Christian bases for involvement with environmental concerns.

A practical basis

Soon after the first manned space flights it became popular to speak of 'spaceship Earth' and of the Earth as our 'life-support system'. These are helpful analogies because they are reminders that, like those of a space capsule, the life-supporting resources of the Earth *are* limited. Let us take some examples.

1. If we continue using oil and natural gas at our present rate, the known resources will run out within about fifty years.

2. The ozone layer, vital for the protection of life against cancer-inducing radiation, is being destroyed by the gases manufactured for use in refrigerators and aerosol spray cans.

3. The tropical rain forests are being rapidly destroyed when we have only just begun to explore their rich resources of plant and animal life – such as the Madagascan primrose, which has yielded an anti-cancer drug.

4. After some years of careful study and debate, the prestigious Inter-Governmental Panel on Climate Change has concluded that global warming is a reality and that, as a result, there are going to be major problems over the next several decades as the sea level rises and the pattern of the world's climate changes.

What can be said about this from a biblical Christian perspective?

Christians recognize that the Earth is our God-given life-support system. We do have a God-given right to make use of its resources.[2] But that does not mean that we should condone careless or wasteful use of them. Far from it. One of the virtues commended in that very down-to-earth biblical book, Proverbs, is *prudence*. In Proverbs, two features of prudence are highlighted: 'The prudent [man] looks where he is going' (14:15); and 'A prudent man sees danger and hides himself' (22:3). These proverbs encourage us to look ahead and take thought for the future consequences of our actions, and not simply to do what is advantageous in the short term. Also we are to anticipate and prepare for danger. Both of these are very ecologically sound precepts. In the light of this, it is not surprising to find that in the Law of Moses there are laws about land use which are clearly intended to ensure sustainable use of the land for agriculture.[3]

A moral basis

Jesus summed up the basis of Christian morality in the two-fold command to love God with all our being, and to love our neighbour as ourselves.[4] We shall return to the implications of loving God later, and consider at this point the implications for environmental concern of the command to love our neighbour as ourselves.

Whenever there is a planning inquiry about something like building a new power station, the route of a new bypass or the siting of a sewage-treatment plant, what is called the 'NIMBY factor' arises – 'not in my back yard'. Now if we do not want one of these in our back yard, why should we impose it on anyone else? Did not Jesus say, 'As you wish that men would do to you, do so to them' (Luke 6:31)? Surely loving our neighbour as ourselves means being prepared to work for the best solution for both parties: using less energy so that the new power station is not needed, urging the government to adopt a transport policy which encourages greater use of public transport and reduces the use of private cars so that new roads are not needed, and so on.

Most of the time we think of our neighbours in spatial terms, as those who live in our road, our town, our country (and maybe even our world). But we also have neighbours in time, our children and our grandchildren. The Bible lays some stress on responsibility to future generations.[5] What kind of world are we passing on to them? Surely it is not loving them to pass on a world of greatly depleted natural resources, polluted by our waste products, and threatened with major climate changes due to global warming?

Although the Bible clearly does put humans in a different category from other creatures, we alone being made in the image of God, this does not mean that we can ignore the welfare of non-human creatures.

They share the Earth with us and are 'neighbours' in that sense. There are plenty of indications in the Bible that God takes their welfare seriously. The first covenant mentioned in the Bible, the one that followed Noah's flood, is made with 'every living creature', not just humans.[6] There are laws concerning animal welfare.[7] In the light of these, Proverbs 12:10 comes as no surprise: 'A righteous man has regard for the life of his beast.' And what about Jonah 4:11, where God's concern is not just for the human inhabitants of Nineveh, but also for the animals? All in all, there are strong moral reasons why those who seek to follow Jesus and to take the Bible seriously should get involved in environmental debate and action.

A spiritual basis

Throughout the history of the church, there have been those who have argued that the church should care for and save people's souls and not get involved in politics. However, it is not as simple as that. Politics is about how we order our lives so that we can live together in relative harmony. Christianity is also about how we should live together, on the basis of loving our neighbour as ourselves. The two inevitably interact. The fact is that the way we organize our lives can, and does, affect even people's readiness and ability to hear and respond to God, which they need to do for the good of their souls.

Take a simple example. Looking up at the night sky in ancient Israel, a psalmist felt a sense of God's presence and responded in awe and wonder, bursting into song: 'The heavens are telling the glory of God and the firmament proclaims his handiwork' (Psalm 19:1). The city-dweller looking up at the night sky of Liverpool or London (as I have often done) cannot share that experience, because of the photochemical smog and light pollution blotting out all but the brightest stars. This pollution inflicts a real spiritual deprivation on us. Christians therefore should be concerned about such pollution as an issue relating to the *spiritual* well-being of people, and not only their physical well-being. For the same reason Christians should press for the preservation and restoration of 'wilderness areas', where people can experience at first hand the presence of God in the created order as the psalmist did. This would, I am sure, help to open up secular people to the reality of the spiritual realm.

A personal basis

The heavens declare the glory of God because they are his 'handiwork', or, as another psalmist puts it, 'the work of [his] fingers' (Psalm 8:3). All craft-workers or artists put something of themselves into what they create. God has done this with his great work of art, the universe in general, and the Earth in particular. We read in Genesis 1 that after each creative act God declared the result to be 'good'. The Hebrew word is used for both moral goodness and aesthetic beauty. Although the original creation was free from the effects of evil, as applied to the non-human creation, the main emphasis must have been on its aesthetic beauty. This tells us that if we love God, and so seek to share God's perspective on things, when evaluating what we do with God's creation we should consider its beauty, because it means so much to God, and we should not let economic values swamp all others.

God's repeated statement that the Earth and its creatures are 'good'. forms an important context for the statement in Genesis 12:26–28 to which critics of Christianity take such exception. They, and even some Christians, are quite wrong to see a licence to exploit and ravage the Earth in the command contained in these verses that we should 'subdue' and 'have dominion over' it. Surely God would not create something beautiful and then command us to despoil and destroy it! Moreover, if we love God we will not want to do that to his precious work of art. This is the Christian's personal motivation for the proper use of the Earth. It has been given to us by the God whom we love and who is very pleased with it. It is God's property, not ours, given to us in trust. We are not the owners but stewards of it. We should want to care for it and develop it in a way that will preserve the goodness of it which made it pleasing to him. There is another aspect of the context of these verses which is also important. The command to 'subdue' and 'have dominion over' the Earth is given to humans only because we are made in the image of God, able to reflect God's character in our own personality. This implies that we ought to obey that command in a way that reflects that character. God acts in ways that are wise, just and loving, and so should we.

Far from giving us a free licence to do what we like with the Earth, Genesis 1:26–28, when properly understood in its context, calls us to act as wise stewards of God's good creation, not just because we are accountable to him as its owner, but particularly because of our respect for it as the handiwork of the one whom we love. This is not a new concept, developed only in the light of the ecological crises of the late twentieth century. John Calvin was advocating it in 1554:

> The Earth was given to man with this condition, that he should occupy himself in its cultivation . . . The custody of the garden was given in charge to Adam, to show that we possess the things that God has committed to our hands, on the condition, that being content with a frugal and moderate use of them, we should take care of what shall remain . . . Let everyone regard himself as the steward of God in all things which he possesses. Then will he neither conduct himself dissolutely, nor corrupt by abuse those things which God requires to be preserved.[8]

The mention of our accountability to God brings me to the biblical teaching about 'the last things', God's ultimate purpose for his creation and his judgment on it.

An eschatological basis

The faith expressed in the Old Testament is a very 'materialistic' one in the sense that, far from there being any rejection of the physical realm as evil, there is a full acceptance of its goodness. After all, did not God himself declare that it is 'good', even 'very good'? It is in accord with this that we find that the future hope of Israel includes the physical world. The world is not to be destroyed but rather to be transformed.[9] The future state of humans is not that of disembodied spirits in heaven, but of resurrected bodies in a re-created heaven and earth.[10] We find the same themes in the New Testament.[11] What is new in the New Testament is the role of Christ as the link between creation and re-creation.[12]

2 Peter 3:8–11, concerning the end of the world, seems to cause some people a problem with regard to environmental concern. If everything is to be burnt up, why bother about conservation today? I think that two points are important here. First, it is unclear how far the language used in this passage is purely metaphorical, signifying God's ultimate act of judgment on the world.[13] Secondly, Peter speaks of new heavens and a new earth. These can be seen as a transformed and purified form of the present heavens and earth. As with our bodies, there will be continuity as well as discontinuity. The fires should probably be seen more as purifying than as destructive.

There is another eschatological factor which we need to take seriously. Colossians 1:16 tells us that the universe, including the Earth, was created 'for him' (i.e. Christ). In Hebrews 1:2, Christ is called the 'heir to all things' which God has created. This Earth is part of Christ's 'inheritance' which he will claim when he comes again at the consummation of God's purposes. Let us extend this metaphor a bit. If someone was left an estate as an inheritance, and appointed trustees to look after it until he could claim it, he would be very upset and angry if he found that they had smashed up the house, concreted the beautiful garden and polluted the lake so that it was a stagnant sewer. How will Christ feel when he comes to receive his inheritance? How will his followers feel about *their* part in caring (or not caring) for it when he receives it?

The highest motive for Christian environmental concern is love for God our Creator and Christ our Saviour. What we do about caring for the Earth is a measure of that love.[14]

CONCLUSIONS

The New Age critique of science

When I give a talk or lecture about the New Age movement, I am usually asked whether I think that it is merely a passing fad. My reply is that, whereas it will no doubt change in various ways, I do not think that it will go away soon. This is because I think we are living through a period of major cultural change in Western society and that the New Age movement reflects this change.

In the brief survey of the New Age movement in the opening chapter, the point was made that it is in large part a reaction against the spiritual aridity that has been an increasing feature of Western culture over the last two centuries. A growing materialism and secularism have marginalized things spiritual, so that they are at best ignored, and at worse denied any reality. There have been protests against this before. Some examples are the Romantic movement in the early nineteenth century, the rise of theosophy at the turn of the century, and the counter-culture movement in the 1960s. However, these were largely isolated movements limited in their appeal and effect, though the last two did prepare the way for what we are seeing today. The difference now is that there is a general breaking-down in Western culture of certainties that arose after the Enlightenment, with the result that we are entering a new era, so-called 'post-modernism'.[1] The rise of the New Age movement is part of this wider cultural change. If Christians are to communicate effectively in this new situation, they must be aware of, and understand, what is going on around them and discern how the Christian good news applies to it.

One of the marks of culture since the Enlightenment has been confidence in the power of analytical reasoning to get to 'the truth' about life, the universe and everything. The form of analytical reasoning which came to be adopted as the universal paradigm – to be idolized, one might say – was that used in the physical sciences, or, more correctly, an idealized version of that form. Because the physical sciences are concerned only with matter and energy (which we now know are inter-convertible) and with the interactions between different forms of matter and energy, they are inherently materialistic, and this limitation tended to be taken over into other disciplines. Perhaps the clearest example of where this leads was seen in logical positivism.[2] According to the logical positivists, the only *meaningful* statements are tautologies (statements that are true by definition of their terms) or 'empirically verifiable statements' (those that can be proved scientifically). This ruled out as *meaningless* vast areas of human language and the experiences to which it refers, including aesthetics, morality and religion. Logical positivism has now faded away as a major philosophy, partly because its basic axiomatic statement that 'the only meaningful synthetic statements are those that are empirically verifiable' is itself not empirically verifiable. It does, however, illustrate the ethos of Western culture in the twentieth century, in its implicit denigration of matters moral and spiritual.

To some extent, the criticisms which New Age adherents make of Western culture echo what some Christians have been saying for a long time. However, Christians need to be discriminating here. In their reaction against Western rationalism, New Agers, as we have seen, tend to subordinate rationality to intuition or to mystical ways of knowing. It will be argued below that a biblical Christianity, while rejecting the idolizing of human reason, leads to a more positive attitude towards the place of rationality in seeking and discovering truth than is found in New Age circles.

A manifestation of the analytical side of scientific reasoning is the reductionist methodology, which was discussed briefly in the context of the New Age attitude to physics (see pages 58–60). Again, it was pointed out then that, while Christians have a good deal of sympathy with the New Age critique, having voiced similar protests in the past,[3] they see New Agers going too far in failing to distinguish between reductionism as a *methodology* and as a *metaphysical stance*. It is worth expanding a little on what was said above about there being evidence from within science itself of the limitations of a reductionist methodology. Arthur Peacocke points out that there are scientific theories and concepts which are essential for understanding systems at a particular level of complexity, but which have no place at the lower level that results when the system is taken apart, and which cannot be explained by the theories that apply at the lower level.[4] An example of this is the 'genetic code' by means of which the information necessary for the making and sustaining of a living cell is stored in its genetic 'data bank', the DNA molecule. DNA has been analysed into the chemical molecules of which it is made, and they of course are made up of different atoms. As a result we can understand how the structure of DNA makes the genetic code *possible*, but there is nothing inherent in the physics and chemistry of its constituents that can explain the actual nature of the code, or why there is a code at all. This means that cell biochemistry can never be 'reduced' simply to physics and chemistry. There is something about the cell as a whole that is more than the sum of the chemicals of which it is made. This kind of example, Peacocke argues, shows that as systems increase in complexity, truly novel phenomena appear which cannot be explained in a reductionist way. The whole *is* more than the sum of the parts. Nevertheless, it is still valid, and valuable, to study the parts, as long as it is remembered that this gives an incomplete picture of the whole. The result is a 'multi-layered' view of reality in which there is recognition of the need for, and validity of, different kinds of explanations at different levels of complexity. In the case of human beings these will include the biochemical, the physiological, the psychological, the social and the spiritual.

The New Age appeal to science

The assumption that the success of reductionist methodology proves the validity of metaphysical reductionism is an example of a common error: the facile shift from physics, or any other branch of science, to metaphysics without justifying the move. One would expect there to be some correlation between metaphysics and the way the physical world is and operates. Some metaphysical stances may be quite incompatible with particular physical realities. However, the correlation may well be far from simple, and the way that the physical world is may be compatible with more than one metaphysical stance.

Perhaps it is because New Agers do not spot the fallacy involved in the simplistic move from science to metaphysics in the reductionists, whom they criticize, that they fall into the same kind of error themselves. We have pointed out this error above, especially in connection with their appeal to the new physics and their use of the Gaia hypothesis (see chapters 4 and 10). It is clearly seen, for example, in their unjustified assumption that the *physical* energy that physicists study is one and the same thing as the *psychic* or *spiritual* energy about which the mystics speak. We have argued that this error is compounded by three others. The first is the appeal to controversial understandings of science (quantum theory and the Gaia hypothesis), without any recognition that they are controversial. Secondly, their appeal to science is sometimes patently false, such as the claim that the equivalence of matter and energy means that matter is an illusion. Finally, there is the fact that the appeal to Eastern mystical thought is selective and often involves a misunderstanding of what the mystics actually mean by the terms they use.

We have also argued that a New Age interpretation of the mystical experience of the unity of the cosmos and oneness with it in terms of a monistic metaphysics is not a necessary one. In fact it is a questionable one, since it leads to a denial as illusory of our 'normal' experience of the diversity of the cosmos.

The New Age concept of God

Because of their monistic outlook, when New Agers have a concept of God it is a pantheistic one. God and the cosmos are identified with each other. In the discussion of New Age spirituality and ecology, two problems with this view were pointed out. One is that it removes the is/ought tension which is the basis for moral action. It is the intuition or belief that things *ought* to be different from the way they currently *are* that leads people to say that something is *wrong* and to take action to change things. If God, the ultimate source of meaning and value, is one with the cosmos, the way things are is the way they ought to be. As a result, evil stops being something objective and simply becomes the result of our distorted vision of things. What needs changing is our understanding of reality. The solution is to be found in education and enlightenment. This, of course, is the classical view of evil in the Eastern religions. When, despite it, adherents of these religions do try to change the way things are, rather than just their view of them, they are showing that there is something problematic in this view of evil.

Pantheism also denies any qualitative difference between humans and non-human entities. All are expressions, though perhaps in differing degrees, of the one divine ultimate reality. Pantheism also calls into question, and for some is taken to deny, the reality of our perception of individual personhood. We are all part of an undivided whole. That ultimate oneness is sometimes conceived of as a cosmic consciousness, but even so it is hard to think of the cosmos as a personal being. As a result, the reality of personhood is called into question also. We shall show below that a trinitarian concept of God gives a more satisfactory account of our experience of humanness.

Process theology

Rupert Sheldrake, standing on the fringe of the New Age movement, adopts the panentheistic concept of God put forward by process theologians.[5] According to this view, the cosmos is dependent on God and is 'in God', but God transcends the cosmos and is not to be simply equated with it. However, God does depend on there being a cosmos, and constantly interacts with it. Moreover, in this view, God is seen not as omniscient and omnipotent, but as developing along with the cosmos as it passes through its history.

This is not the place to enter into a detailed discussion and critique of process theology.[6] Just a brief survey will have to suffice. Classical Western philosophy and, following it, much Western theology have worked with a distinction between the states of 'being' and 'becoming'. Ultimate reality has been seen as a state of 'being' and the Perfect Being (God) as totally unchanging 'substance'. There are problems when one tries to relate this view of God to the God of the Bible who interacts with the world and, in particular, who enters into a loving relationship with created human beings. However, process thought faces some major problems too.

Process philosophy makes 'becoming' the ultimate reality. Reality is a sequence of events. Any concept of an enduring substance, be it an atom, or a person, or God, is an abstraction. But how is the sequence of events tied together? The answer is that each event builds upon preceding events and is partly determined by them. However, each new event is also partly free to determine itself. This talk of events 'determining' themselves makes process thought 'panpsychic'. From every level, from sub-atomic particle to God, there is some sense (appropriate to the kind of event) in which an event can 'remember' the events in its past and can 'determine' itself.

Perhaps the attraction of process philosophy for theologians is that such a system requires a 'God' to perform two essential functions. First, by experiencing and remembering the whole of reality, God gives it unity and cohesion. Secondly, God envisages all the possibilities open to the process and so can 'offer' them as appropriate to each event. This God, by combining memory of the past and possibilities for the future, provides an ever-enriched store of 'material' on which the process may draw as it moves through time. God moves through time with the process becoming enriched by it as the universe proceeds.

What emerges from this is what is called the 'bipolar' view of God. On the one hand, God has a 'concrete pole' or 'consequent nature' which is fully involved in the process of the universe and so is changeable, passive, unsure of the future. On the other hand, in order to avoid collapse into pantheism and to provide the 'pure possibilities' for the future, God must have an 'abstract pole' or 'conceptual nature' which is separate from the universe and is unchanging and all-knowing.

Process theology faces two kinds of problem. First, there are problems which are internal to it. Is it logically coherent? Is the concept of a bipolar God simply paradoxical or is it logically incoherent? Many Christian theologians, and non-Christian philosophers, find it logically incoherent. As a result, as Gunton points out,[7] the hope that it would act as a bridge between secular and religious thought has been dashed, since few, if any, secular philosophers take it seriously.

Secondly, the compatibility of process theology with Christian theology is very debatable. I can briefly mention only a few difficulties.

1. It is hard to relate the bipolar God of process thought with the trinitarianism of historic Christianity. One might equate God the Father with the abstract pole, and God the Spirit with the concrete pole, but where does God the Son fit in? This leads us to the next point.

2. Process theologians tend not to speak of either the Holy Spirit or God the Son, but of the Logos as the symbol of God relating to the world. Who, or what, then, is Jesus? He is the fullest incarnation of the Logos, or the person (a series of events, remember) who was most open to (most influenced by) the Logos (God's influence in the world). This, however, tends to make Jesus different from other creatures only in *degree*, not in *kind*, and is certainly not an expression of the traditional doctrine of the incarnation.

3. In process thought, God's action in the world is no more than 'influence'. God 'lures' events towards a particular goal. God is always essentially passive with respect to the world. This seems to leave little room for what is at the heart of the biblical good news: God's great initiatives of grace, the kingdom that broke into the world, the love that actively seeks the lost and judges those who reject it, and the power that raises the dead.

4. Following on from this, process theology has problems in finding any room for a real act of redemption in Jesus. Process thought is essentially optimistic but non-eschatological. The self-enriching process is the ultimate 'good' and will go on eternally. My life will, inescapably,

have an everlasting effect on that process. The best I can hope for is that it should be a 'good' effect (however that is defined). It is hard to see where there is room, or need, for any kind of redemption and personal forgiveness of sins. The cross becomes simply a symbol of God's willingness to accept past evil and to transform it into good.

Given these problems, it is not surprising to find Gunton concluding that the process concept of God 'is Procrustean, in that it makes it impossible to say many of the things that Christian theology has wanted to say about God' and that 'the Gospel cannot bear the changes that appear to be required and remain the Christian Gospel'.[8] Lawrence Osborn says much the same: 'Process metaphysics becomes a bed of Procrustes on which Biblical Christianity is stretched beyond recognition'.[9]

Faced with such problems, it seems preferable to find ways of re-expressing theism to meet the weaknesses in it which are highlighted by the process theologians than to adopt process theology.

A trinitarian epilogue

Although pantheism is thought of as characteristic of the Eastern religions, it is not new to the West. The early Christian theologians had to face it, especially in the guise of Graeco-Roman Stoicism. The doctrine of 'creation out of nothing' was formulated as a biblical response to it. In saying that God created the world 'out of nothing' they were making the following affirmations.

1. God is the only self-existent entity. He does not depend on the universe for his existence and is not to be identified with the universe.

2. The universe does depend on God for both the origin of its existence and its continuance in being.

3. There is a sharp, clear difference between Creator and creation. The two are not to be confused.

This last point is important for modern science. Colin Russell,[10] among other historians of science, points out the link between the rise of modern science and the de-deification of nature, which he attributes to the increasing influence of a biblical theology freed from Aristotelianism in the seventeenth century. To return to a pantheistic world-view, with its view of the Earth as a divine or semi-divine organism, would be to undermine one of the bases of the modern scientific enterprise.

The doctrine of 'creation out of nothing' stresses the transcendence of God over the creation. However, this is not to be pushed to the extreme of what is called 'deism', the teaching that, once the world had been created, God left it alone to get on by itself with no reference to, or involvement with, himself. The Bible balances the teaching about God's transcendence with an insistence on God's immanence, God's active involvement in and with the creation, and in and with his human creatures in history. It is here that the doctrine of God as Trinity is so important. It enables us to hold together God's transcendence and immanence. The doctrine asserts that God is a unity, but not a monistic, undifferentiated unity. Rather, within God, there is the unity of harmonious, differentiated relationships and activity. In particular, as Father, God is the Creator who is transcendent over his creation but, as Spirit, God is the immanent Creator constantly at work in the world.

The doctrine of the Trinity also enables Christians to hold to both the reality of the diversity of the created cosmos and the inter-dependence and unity of its many parts. Both the diversity and the unity have their ground in the nature of God, the ultimate reality. It is important to say, however, that the doctrine of the Trinity was not an abstract idea devised to solve some philosophical problems. It arose out of the desire to be true to the revelation of God in the historical person of Jesus of Nazareth, in the Christian Scriptures (which include the record of the birth, life, death and resurrection of Jesus), and in the continuing Christian experience of God.

Human beings are special creatures, made in the image of God. The full meaning of this has been much discussed by Christian theologians. At the very least it means that the human personality is capable of expressing, in a finite, and so limited, way something of the character of God. As a result we are able to enter into a personal relationship with God. Moreover, far from denying the reality of individual human persons, we are made in the image of a God who is triune, in whom there is a harmonious inter-relationship of persons. Christians can affirm this, while also affirming the need for humans to live together in harmonious relationships in order to be fully human. These relationships are made possible by self-giving love such as that evidenced in Jesus' life and death, and made real in our lives by the work of God the Spirit.

The distinction between Creator and creation enables Christians to hold firm to the insight that this is a fallen creation in which created beings have used the freedom God gave them to disobey their Creator and go their own way in opposition to his purposes. Hence evil can be taken seriously as a reality, not just an illusion. The is/ought distinction is important. In so many situations we cannot accept the way things are, but know that they ought to be changed for the better, and that they can be with God's help. God is at work redeeming and restoring this fallen creation. The ultimate end of God's purpose is not a state of immaterial, unified, undifferentiated consciousness. It is the beauty of a harmonious but highly differentiated new heaven and new earth, inhabited by human beings in resurrection bodies restored to a proper relationship with God. Jesus plays a pivotal role in this work of redemption and restoration. In him, God the Son entered into the fallen creation and did battle with evil, overcoming it and securing redemption by his obedient life, his sacrificial death and his glorious resurrection.

This Christian world-view, sketched only briefly above, has implications for our understanding of the scientific enterprise. Because the cosmos is created and sustained by God as an entity distinct from himself, there is a reality 'out there', independent of humans, for the scientist to discover and study. This cosmos, we are told in the Bible, reflects something of God's nature.[11] It is an ordered cosmos,[12] made according to God's wise design.[13] Humans are made in the image of God. As a result we share something of the mind and wisdom of God and so can expect to have at least a limited understanding of the order in the cosmos which God designed. We can share with Johann Kepler the belief that in studying the cosmos we are 'thinking God's thoughts after him'.[14] As we have said before, this knowledge of the cosmos will always be limited and distorted, but we can pursue it in the hope that as our scientific theories are modified and refined, we are getting closer and closer to a true understanding of the reality of the cosmos.

Although the image of God in humans is far more than merely rationality, since it embraces the whole of human personality, there are places in the Bible where rationality is seen as that which distinguishes humans from the animals. A dramatic example is the story of Nebuchadnezzar's madness in Daniel 4, in which, when the king loses human reason, he becomes like 'the beasts of the field'. Another interesting example is Psalm 32:8–9, where knowledge of God's will comes through instruction, teaching and understanding, and this is contrasted with the way animals have to be directed by use of bit and bridle. It is striking that in 1 Corinthians 14:13–19 the apostle Paul insists that in the worship of God the mind should be engaged. There is no place for denigration of rational thought in the Christian tradition.

Does science matter?

What if New Age thinking does become dominant in our culture and we reach 'the end of science' as Zukav thinks we will?[15] Does it matter?

Before answering that, it is worth pointing out to the sceptics that there is at least a partial historical precedent for a change in the dominant outlook on reality having a marked effect on the progress of science. This is the deadening effect which the rise of the Mutakallimum school of philosophy and theology had on the development of science in the Arab world in medieval times.[16]

To return to our question. Would the demise of the scientific enterprise matter? Nearly everyone would feel the force of a positive answer on utilitarian grounds. Few of us would like to live in a world subject to the major epidemics that raged periodically before the discovery of vaccination and antibiotics, and the periodic famines which preceded modern scientific farming. The fact that epidemics and famines do still occur in some places reminds us that the battle against them has not yet been finally won and that they could easily return. We could all write a long list of the benefits of science and technology which we would now be loath to be without. Of course these benefits have also brought problems in the form of pollution, global warming, species extinction, the arms race, depletion of non-renewable resources, unjust distribution of wealth between nations, and the like. Few of those who have given serious thought to the matter, however, believe that we can solve the problems by abandoning science. What is needed is not the end of science, but a better, more humane and environmentally appropriate use of it. At a recent World Environment and Development Conference in London, Dr Sue Mayer, Science Unit Manager for Greenpeace UK, said:

> If science is willing to be open to change in its own culture and institutions, it should maintain an important role in the future and be effectively harnessed for the benefit of society and the environment.[17]

Apart from the utilitarian argument, I think that there are specifically Christian reasons for saying that it does matter whether or not the scientific enterprise continues. I believe that Christians have every reason to be committed to the scientific enterprise. As we have seen, Christian beliefs and motivation played a positive role in the rise of modern science. In his *Institutes of the Christian Religion* John Calvin wrote:

> If we regard the Spirit of God as the sole fountain of truth, we shall neither reject the truth itself, nor despise it wherever it shall appear, unless we wish to dishonour the Spirit of God. For by holding the gifts of the Spirit in slight esteem, we contemn and reproach the Spirit himself.[18]

The editors of the Library of Christian Classics edition entitle the section in which the statement occurs 'Science as God's Gift'. I think that they have rightly understood the implications of the truth which Calvin expresses. Disciples of Jesus, who described himself as 'the truth' (John 14:6) and who promised to send to his disciples the Spirit of truth (John 15:26), ought to be concerned to safeguard one of the important ways in which we can discover truth, in particular the truth about what Francis Bacon called 'the book of God's works'.[19]

Truth has value in itself. It is part of our human make-up, being the image of God, that we can delight simply in the discovery and grasping of the truth. Truth can also have practical value. Bacon, like many of the early modern scientists, was motivated by the belief that what we would now call science and technology was a gift of God by means of which the effects of the fall can be at least partially repaired in this life.[20] For the Christian, the truth which science discovers is not just useful knowledge about God's world. It also tells us something about God, and so enriches our spiritual life and inspires our worship of God. In fact, the scientific enterprise is one way of fulfilling the double command to love God with all our being and our neighbour as ourselves (Mk. 12:28–31).

Conclusion

It seems appropriate to end with some words from one of the founders of modern science, who in his own personal pilgrimage moved from an animistic understanding of the cosmos to a de-deified one[21] – Johann Kepler. The following quotation, in which he explains why he was willing to spend some five years looking for the correct geometrical shape for the orbit of Mars, shows how his thinking was formed by biblical theology:

> Geometry existed before the creation, is co-eternal with the mind of God, is God himself (what exists in God that is not God himself?), geometry provided God with a model for the creation and was implanted into man, together with God's own likeness – not merely converged to his mind through the eyes.[22]

Here Kepler is writing not as a systematic theologian, but as an astronomer who is excited by his discoveries – the laws of planetary motion. His language is imprecise. Judged by the standards of systematic theology, what he says about geometry might at first seem almost heretical from an orthodox Christian standpoint. However, taken in its own terms, I do not think it is – at least, no more so than the pictorial language used in Proverbs 8:22–31. This passage speaks of wisdom, in personified terms, being with God long before the creation of the Earth and playing the role of master worker, or perhaps architect, in the creation of the heavens and the earth.[23] If 'geometry' is replaced by 'wisdom' (of which it is an aspect), it is clear that Kepler is echoing Proverbs 8:22–31 and 3:19–20 in the first part of the quotation. The second half clearly relies on Genesis 1:26–28. The point he is making is that the order we see in creation is not merely an invention of our minds. This order was put there by God, and we can discover it and understand it because we are made in God's image. Kepler has clearly derived this from the Bible.

The prayer of thanks that Kepler offers to God is one which all Christians involved in science could make their own:

I give you thanks, Creator and God, that you have given me this joy in your creation, and I rejoice in the works of your hands. See I have now completed the work to which I was called. In it I have used the talents you have lent to my spirit. I have revealed the majesty of your works to those who will read my words, insofar as my narrow understanding can comprehend their infinite richness.[24]

NOTES

In quotations, all italicization of words or phrases follows the italicization of the original works.

Introduction

1. A good, short, readable introduction is provided by J. C. Polkinghorne, *Quarks, Chaos and Christianity* (Triangle, 1994). A more detailed but still very readable treatment is J. Houghton, *The Search for God: Can Science Help?* (Lion, 1995).

1. What is the New Age movement?

1. E. Miller, *A Crash Course on the New Age Movement* (Monarch, 1990). Appendix B has a detailed critique of Constance Cumbey's claim that the movement is an organized conspiracy.
2. *Ibid.*, p. 15.
3. Quoted in M. Cole *et al.*, *What is the New Age?* (Hodder & Stoughton, 1990), p. 6.
4. Miller, *A Crash Course in the New Age Movement*, p. 24.
5. For a discussion of the reason for the Sun's movement and the differences among astrologers over the date of the beginning of the

Age of Aquarius, see R. B. Culver and P. A. Ianna, *Astrology: True or False?* (Prometheus Books, 1988), pp. 67–82.

6. F. Capra, *The Turning Point* (Flamingo, 1982), p. 410.
7. S. MacLaine, *It's All in the Playing* (Bantam, 1986), p. 172.
8. E. Caddy, *Dawn of Change* (Findhorn Press, 1979), p. 1.
9. J. Underhill, 'New Age Quiz', *Life Times* 3, p. 6, quoted in R. Chandler, *Understanding the New Age* (Milton Keynes: Word UK, 1989), pp. 28f.
10. C. Riddell, *The Findhorn Community* (Findhorn Press, 1990), p. 30.
11. *Ibid.*
12. Cited in G. Melton (ed.), *New Age Encyclopedia* (Gale Research, 1990), p. 133.
13. M. Ferguson, *The Aquarian Conspiracy* (Paladin, 1982).
14. Riddell, *The Findhorn Community*, p. 25.
15. S. MacLaine, *Dancing in the Light* (Bantam, 1986), p. 109.
16. MacLaine, *It's All in the Playing*, p. 174.
17. Cited in *New Age Encyclopedia*, p. 324.
18. Riddell, *The Findhorn Community*, p. 29.
19. For a detailed account of, and response to, New Age teaching about Jesus, see D. Groothuis, *Revealing the New Age Jesus* (IVP, 1990).
20. S. MacLaine, *Out on a Limb* (Elm Tree, 1983), p. 209.

2. Science and knowledge in the New Age

1. R. Storm, *In Search of Heaven on Earth* (Bloomsbury, 1991), p. 191.
2. W. H. Newton-Smith, *The Rationality of Science* (Routledge & Kegan Paul, 1986), p. 1.
3. P. K. Feyerabend, *Against Method* (New Left Books, 1975).
4. T. S. Kuhn, *The Structure of Scientific Revolutions*, 2nd edn (Chicago University Press, 1970).
5. T. Roszak, *The Making of a Counter Culture* (Anchor, 1969), p. 208.
6. Rajneesh, *I Am the Gate* (Harper & Row, 1977), p. 18.
7. R. E. Ornstein, *The Psychology of Consciousness* (W. H. Freeman, 1973). For a popular account, see R. E. Ornstein and R. E. Thompson,

The Amazing Brain (Chatto & Windus, 1985), esp. pp. 151–171.

8. M. Kinsbourne (ed.), *Asymmetrical Function of the Brain* (CUP, 1978).
9. M. Ferguson, *The Aquarian Conspiracy* (Paladin, 1982), p. 83.
10. *Ibid.*, pp. 84f.
11. F. Capra, *The Tao of Physics* (Flamingo, 1983), p. 37.
12. F. Capra, *The Turning Point* (Flamingo, 1985), ch. 2.
13. Capra, *The Tao of Physics*, pp. 52f.
14. *Ibid.*, pp. 30f.
15. G. Zukav, *The Dancing Wu Li Masters* (Flamingo, 1989), p. 331.
16. G. F. Chew, quoted in Zukav, *The Dancing Wu Li Masters*, p. 331.
17. Ferguson, *The Aquarian Conspiracy*, p. 160.
18. *Ibid.*, p. 157.
19. Capra, *The Tao of Physics*, p. 30.
20. See S. MacLaine, *Dancing in the Light* (Bantam, 1986), pp. 337f.
21. Capra, *The Tao of Physics*, p. 30.

3. The new physics and New Age thought

1. Lord Kelvin (William Thompson), 'Nineteenth Century Clouds over the Dynamical Theory of Heat and Light', *Philosophical Magazine* 2 (1901), pp. 1–40.
2. For an introduction to the theory of relativity, see J. A. Coleman, *Relativity for the Layman* (Penguin, 1966).
3. For an introduction to quantum theory, see J. C. Polkinghorne, *The Quantum World* (Penguin, 1986).
4. F. Capra, *The Tao of Physics* (Flamingo, 1986), p. 227.
5. G. Zukav, *The Dancing Wu Li Masters* (Flamingo, 1989), p. 177.
6. Capra, *The Tao of Physics*, p. 226.
7. Zukav, *The Dancing Wu Li Masters*, p. 219.
8. Capra, *The Tao of Physics*, p. 247.
9. H. Zimmer, *Myths and Symbols in Indian Art and Civilisation* (Princeton University Press, 1972), p. 155.
10. Capra, *The Tao of Physics*, p. 272.
11. J. C. Polkinghorne, *One World* (SPCK, 1986), pp. 84, 108.
12. Zukav, *The Dancing Wu Li Masters*, p. 315.

13. *Ibid.*, p. 172.
14. Capra, *The Tao of Physics*, p. 183.
15. *Ibid.*, p. 189.
16. R. K. Clifton and M. G. Regehr, 'Capra on Eastern Mysticism and Modern Physics', *Science and Christian Belief* 1 (1989), pp. 63–66.
17. Capra, *The Tao of Physics*, p. 205.
18. M. Ferguson, *The Aquarian Conspiracy* (Paladin, 1982), p. 182.
19. M. Talbot, *The Holographic Universe* (Grafton, 1991).
20. F. Capra, *The Turning Point* (Flamingo, 1985), p. 77.
21. M. Talbot, *Mysticism and the New Physics* (Routledge & Kegan Paul, 1981), p. 42.
22. S. MacLaine, *Dancing in the Light* (Bantam, 1986), p. 337.
23. *Ibid.*, p. 420.
24. For a rather more detailed discussion, see Clifton and Regehr, 'Capra on Eastern Mysticism and Modern Physics', pp. 57–63; Polkinghorne, *The Quantum World*, pp. 63–69.
25. Capra, *The Tao of Physics*, pp. 78f.
26. *Ibid.*, p. 154.
27. Clifton and Regehr, 'Capra on Eastern Mysticism and Modern Physics', p. 72.
28. For a brief discussion of the definition and nature of logic, see R. H. Popkin and A. Stroll, *Philosophy Made Simple* (W. H. Allen, 1973), pp. 224–228.
29. G. Birkhoff and J. von Neumann, 'The Logic of Quantum Mechanics', *Annals of Mathematics* (1936), p. 37.
30. D. Finkelstein, at an Esalen Conference on Physics and Consciousness, Big Sur, California, 1976. Quoted in Zukav, *The Dancing Wu Li Masters*, p. 284.
31. D. Finkelstein, quoted in Zukav, *The Dancing Wu Li Masters*, p. 277.
32. P. Gibbins, *Particles and Paradoxes* (CUP, 1987), pp. 142f.

4. Physics and Eastern mysticism

1. R. H. Jones, *Science and Mysticism* (Associated University Presses, 1986), p. 204.

2. *Ibid.*, pp. 184, 202.
3. *Ibid.*, p. 202.
4. *Ibid.*, pp. 204ff.
5. *Ibid.*, pp. 185f.
6. *Ibid.*, pp. 192–194.
7. A. Peacocke, *God and the New Biology* (Dent & Sons, 1986), chs. 1 and 2.
8. H. Wheeler Robinson, *The Christian Doctrine of Man*, 3rd edn (T. & T. Clark, 1947), p. 27.
9. See, for example, J. H. Brooke, *Science and Religion: Some Historical Perspectives* (CUP, 1991); R. Hooykaas, *Religion and the Rise of Modern Science* (Scottish Academic Press, 1972); S. Jaki, *Science and Creation* (Scottish Academic Press, 1974); C. Russell, *Cross-Currents: Interactions between Science and Faith* (IVP, 1985).
10. P. Helm (ed.), *Objective Knowledge: A Christian Perspective* (IVP, 1987), contains a collection of essays which are very relevant to this paragraph.
11. G. Zukav, *The Dancing Wu Li Masters* (Flamingo, 1989), p. 331.

5. Pierre Teilhard de Chardin and New Age thought

1. M. Ferguson, *The Aquarian Conspiracy* (Paladin, 1982), pp. 460–463.
2. *Ibid.*, p. 19.
3. *Ibid.*, p. 26.
4. F. Capra, *The Turning Point* (Flamingo, 1985), p. 332.
5. Quoted in B. Towers, *Teilhard de Chardin* (John Knox Press, 1966), p. 2.
6. Quoted in *ibid.*, p. 1.
7. Quoted in *ibid.*, pp. 9f.
8. Teilhard's thoughts at this time were expressed in a series of essays, later published as *Writings in Time of War* (Collins, 1968).
9. P. Teilhard de Chardin, *Letters to Léontine Zanta* (Collins, 1968), p. 52.
10. Quoted in C. Cuénot, *Teilhard de Chardin: A Biographical Study* (Burns & Oates, 1965), p. 50.

11. P. Teilhard de Chardin, *Le Milieu divin* (Fontana, 1964), p. 46.

12. Towers, *Teilhard de Chardin*, pp. 43, 45.

13. A. Hanson (ed.), *Teilhard Reassessed* (Darton, Longman & Todd, 1970), pp. viif.

14. In what follows, I am indebted to the summaries of Teilhard's ideas in the following two books (the first by a strong supporter of Teilhard, the second by a critic): Towers, *Teilhard de Chardin*, pp. 27–40; and D. G. Jones, *Teilhard de Chardin: An Analysis and Assessment* (Tyndale Press, 1969), pp. 19–27.

15. Towers, *Teilhard de Chardin*, p. 28.

16. P. Teilhard de Chardin, *The Phenomenon of Man* (Collins, 1963), p. 233.

17. *Ibid.*, p. 249.

18. H. A. Blair, 'Progress', in Hanson (ed.), *Teilhard Reassessed*, p. 81.

19. Teilhard, *The Phenomenon of Man*, p. 288.

20. *Ibid.*, pp. 300–302.

21. *Ibid.*, pp. 53–61.

22. *Ibid.*, pp. 64f.

23. *Ibid.*, p. 233.

24. *Ibid.*, p. 264.

25. *Ibid.*, p. 78.

26. *Ibid.*, p. 102.

27. *Ibid.*, pp. 164f.

28. *Ibid.*, pp. 165f.

29. *Ibid.*, pp. 168f.

30. *Ibid.*, p. 259.

31. *Ibid.*, pp. 269f.

32. *Ibid.*, p. 294.

33. *Ibid.*, p. 297.

34. *Ibid.*, pp. 309f.

35. See, for example, R. B. Smith, 'God and Evolutive Creation', in Hanson (ed.), *Teilhard Reassessed*, pp. 41–58.

36. Capra, *The Turning Point*, p. 332.

37. *Ibid.*

38. Ferguson, *The Aquarian Conspiracy*, pp. 51–53, 307.

39. Quoted by B. de Solages, *Teilhard de Chardin* (Privat, 1967), p. 227 n.

40. Teilhard, *The Phenomenon of Man*, pp. 311–313. R. B. Smith, 'The Place of Evil in a World of Evolution', in Hanson (ed.), *Teilhard Reassessed*, p. 64, presents another discussion of evil from one of Teilhard's other works which gives more attention to specifically human evil.

41. Quoted by Smith, 'The Place of Evil in a World of Evolution', p. 61.

42. *Ibid.*, pp. 70f.

43. Teilhard, *The Phenomenon of Man*, pp. 31–36.

44. Ferguson, *The Aquarian Conspiracy*, p. 71.

45. V. Mangalwadi, *In Search of Self* (Spire, 1992), p. 13.

6. A critique of *The Phenomenon of Man*

1. P. Teilhard de Chardin, *The Phenomenon of Man* (Collins, 1963), p. 29.

2. *Ibid.*, p. 21.

3. P. Medawar, 'Critical Note', *Mind* 70 (1961), p. 99.

4. F. A. Turk, 'The Idea of Biological and Social Progress in the System of Pierre Teilhard de Chardin', in A. Hanson (ed.), *Teilhard Reassessed* (Darton, Longman and Todd, 1970), p. 1, n. 1.

5. See, for example, the more technical articles reprinted in P. Teilhard de Chardin, *The Appearance of Man* (Collins, 1965).

6. Teilhard, *The Phenomenon of Man*, p. 284.

7. *Ibid.*, pp. 254f.

8. *Ibid.*, p. 284.

9. D. G. Jones, *Teilhard de Chardin: An Analysis and Assessment* (Tyndale Press, 1969), p. 31.

10. Teilhard, *The Phenomenon of Man*, p. 30.

11. J. Needham, 'Cosmologist of the Future', *New Statesman*, 7 November 1959, pp. 632f.

12. Teilhard, *The Phenomenon of Man*, p. 150.

13. *Ibid.*, pp. 148–150, 307f.

14. *Ibid.*, p. 138.

15. *Ibid.*, p. 149.

16. *Ibid.*, p. 149, n. 1.

17. Jones, *Teilhard de Chardin*, p. 38.

18. A. R. Peacocke, *Creation and the World of Science* (OUP, 1979), pp. 112–131.
19. N. M . Wildiers, *An Introduction to Teilhard de Chardin* (Collins, 1968), p. 79.
20. J. Huxley in Teilhard, *The Phenomenon of Man*, p. 19.
21. R. B. Smith, 'God and Evolutive Creation', in Hanson (ed.), *Teilhard Reassessed*, p. 43.

7. Biology and New Age thought

1. F. Capra, *The Turning Point* (Flamingo, 1985), pp. 285–332.
2. *Ibid.*, pp. 286f.
3. *Ibid.*, p. 287.
4. *Ibid.*, p. 290.
5. *Ibid.*, p. 303.
6. *Ibid.*, pp. 290f.
7. *Ibid.*, p. 291.
8. *Ibid.*, p. 305.
9. P. A. Weiss, *Within the Gates of Science and Beyond* (Hafner, 1973), p. 276.
10. Capra, *The Turning Point*, p. 305.
11. *Ibid.*, p. 309.
12. See, for example, *The Oxford English Dictionary*.
13. E. Jantsch, *The Self-Organizing Universe* (Pergamon, 1979).
14. Capra, *The Turning Point*, pp. 310f.
15. *Ibid.*, p. 312.
16. *Ibid.*
17. *Ibid.*, p. 313.
18. *Ibid.*, p. 315.
19. *Ibid.*
20. *Ibid.*, p. 322.
21. *Ibid.*, p. 324.
22. *Ibid.*, p. 322.
23. For an introduction to Jung's ideas, see F. Fordham, *An Introduction to Jung's Psychology* (Penguin, 1972).

24. Capra, *The Turning Point*, p. 317.
25. Jantsch, *The Self-Organizing Universe*, p. 308.
26. For this distinction, see p. 58 above.
27. Here Paul's quotation is from a poem attributed to Epimenides the Cretan.

8. A new science of life

1. L. Osborn, *Angels of Light?* (Daybreak, 1992), p. 88.
2. R. Sheldrake, *A New Science of Life* (Blond & Briggs, 1981).
3. D. Summerbell, review of Sheldrake's *A New Science of Life* in *The Biologist*, November 1981, quoted in Sheldrake, *A New Science of Life*, 2nd edn.
4. J. Maddox, Editorial in *Nature*, 24 September 1981.
5. BBC2 television, *Heretic*, 10 pm, 19 July 1994.
6. R. Sheldrake, *A New Science of Life*, 2nd edn (Paladin, 1987), pp. 23–25.
7. *Ibid.*, pp. 53–57.
8. C. H. Waddington, *The Strategy of the Genes* (Allen & Unwin, 1957).
9. Sheldrake, *A New Science of Life*, p. 75.
10. *Ibid.*, p. 76.
11. *Ibid.*, p. 77.
12. *Ibid.*, pp. 79–81.
13. *Ibid.*, p. 96.
14. *Ibid.*, p. 99.
15. *Ibid.*, p. 96.
16. *Ibid.*, p. 114.
17. *Ibid.*, p. 121.
18. *Ibid.*, p. 164.
19. *Ibid.*, pp. 172–179.
20. *Ibid.*, pp. 179–184.
21. *Ibid.*, p. 136.
22. *Ibid.*, pp. 136f.
23. The wider implications of Sheldrake's theory, beyond morphogenesis, are developed further in his later book, *The Presence of the Past*

(Collins, 1988).

24. L. Wolpert, 'A Matter of Fact or Fancy?', *The Guardian*, 11 January 1984.

25. *Ibid.*

26. J. Maddox, *The World Tonight*, BBC Radio 4, 30 October 1981. (Transcript in Sheldrake, *A New Science of Life*, p. 229.) The confidence which Maddox expresses in conventional theories gains some support from a recent article which describes work showing that positional information regarding flowers is encoded in the genes. See E. M. Meyerowitz, 'The Genetics of Flower Development', *Scientific American* 271 (1994), pp. 40–47.

27. C. Tudge, 'Make your own Morphic Resonance Kit', *New Scientist*, 26 March 1994, p. 42.

28. See n. 5 above.

29. Sheldrake, *A New Science of Life*, p. 139.

30. R. Sheldrake, *Seven Experiments that could Change the World* (Fourth Estate, 1994).

31. Sheldrake, *A New Science of Life*, p. 203.

32. *Ibid.*, pp. 203–210.

33. *Ibid.*, p. 209.

34. R. Sheldrake, *The Rebirth of Nature: The Greening of Science and God* (Rider, 1991).

35. *Ibid.*, pp. 154f.

36. *Ibid.*, p. 142.

37. *Ibid.*, p. 146.

38. *Ibid.*, pp. 146f.

39. *Ibid.*, p. 170, quoting from C. Birch and J. B. Cobb, *The Liberation of Life* (CUP, 1981), pp. 196f.

9. The Gaia hypothesis

1. J. Lovelock, *Gaia: A New Look at Life on Earth* (OUP, 1979), pp. 5f.

2. *Ibid.*, p. 39.

3. *Ibid.*, p. 36.

4. L. Margulis, cited in Lovelock, *Gaia*, p. 128.

5. *Ibid.*, p. 11.

6. *Ibid.*

7. J. Lovelock, 'Hands Up for the Gaia Hypothesis', *Nature* 344 (1990), pp. 100–102.

8. J. Lovelock, *The Ages of Gaia: A Biography of our Living Earth* (OUP, 1988), p. 150.

9. Brief summaries and critiques of Popper's ideas are to be found in R. Harré, *The Philosophies of Science*, 2nd edn (OUP, 1985), pp. 49–53, and A. O'Hear, *An Introduction to the Philosophy of Science* (OUP, 1990), pp. 35–53.

10. J. Kirchner, 'Gaia Metaphor Unfalsifiable', *Nature* 345 (1990), p. 470.

11. M. Hesse, *Models and Analogies in Science* (Sheed & Ward, 1963).

12. C. Russell, *The Earth, Humanity and God* (UCL Press, 1994), p. 121.

13. W. F. Doolittle, 'Is Nature Really Motherly?', *CoEvolution Quarterly* 29 (1981), pp. 58–63.

14. R. Dawkins, *The Extended Phenotype* (OUP, 1982).

15. Lovelock, *The Ages of Gaia*, pp. 35–64.

16. *Ibid.*, p. 19.

17. *Ibid.*, pp. 54–57.

18. *Ibid.*, p. 8.

19. *Ibid.*, p. 41.

20. Lovelock, *Gaia*, p. 146.

21. Lovelock, *The Ages of Gaia*, p. 11.

22. *Ibid.*, p. 16.

23. *Ibid.*, p. 17.

24. *Ibid.*, pp. 17–31.

25. L. Margulis, cited in R. Sheldrake, *The Rebirth of Nature* (Rider, 1991), p. 129.

26. Lovelock, 'Hands Up for the Gaia Hypothesis', p. 102.

27. Lovelock, *The Ages of Gaia*, p. 203.

28. Russell, *The Earth, Humanity and God*, pp. 12–18.

29. *Ibid.*, pp. 121f.

30. *Ibid.*, pp. 134f.

31. Lovelock, *The Ages of Gaia*, p. 217.

32. *Ibid.*, p. 206.

33. *Ibid.*
34. *Ibid.*, p. 217.

10. Ecology and New Age spirituality

1. L. White, 'The Historic Roots of our Ecologic Crisis', *Science* 155 (1967), pp. 1203–1207; quotation from p. 1205.
2. K. Pedler, *The Quest for Gaia* (Paladin, 1991), p. 220.
3. F. Capra, *The Tao of Physics* (Flamingo, 1986), p. 11.
4. Pedler, *The Quest for Gaia*, pp. 170f.
5. Cited in D. Burnett, *The Dawning of the Pagan Moon* (MARC, 1991), p. 100.
6. N. Pennick, *Practical Magic in the Northern Tradition* (Aquarian Press, 1989), p. 60.
7. M. Wright, cited in V. Mangalwadi, *In Search of Self* (Spire, 1992), p. 129. Apparently the same approach failed the following year, to Ms Wright's embarrassment.
8. White, 'Historic Roots', p. 1205.
9. C. Russell, *The Earth, Humanity and God* (UCL Press, 1994), p. 88. He gives a detailed response in *Pollution and the Pipes of Pan*, inaugural lecture at the Open University, 10 May 1983.
10. J. Kirby, cited in Burnett, *The Dawning of the Pagan Moon*, pp. 95f.
11. For a recent survey of modern Wicca, see Burnett, *The Dawning of the Pagan Moon*, especially pp. 85–148.
12. V. Crowley, *Wicca: The Old Religion in the New Age* (Aquarian Press, 1989).
13. P. Russell, *The Awakening Earth: The Global Brain* (Routledge & Kegan Paul, 1982).

11. Green Christianity

1. L. White, 'The Historic Roots of our Ecologic Crisis', *Science* 155 (1967), p. 1205.
2. Genesis 1:29; 9:3; Psalm 8:6.

3. For example Deuteronomy 22:6–7; Leviticus 25:1–7.

4. Mark 12:28–34.

5. For example Proverbs 13:22; the laws on sustainable agriculture (see references in n. 3 above).

6. Genesis 9:8–17.

7. For example Exodus 23:4–5; Deuteronomy 22:10; 25:4.

8. J. Calvin, *Commentary on Genesis*, trans. J. King (1847; reprint Banner of Truth, 1965), p. 125.

9. Isaiah 65:17–25.

10. Isaiah 26:19–21.

11. For example Romans 8:18–23; 1 Corinthians 15:35–50.

12. Colossians 1:15–20.

13. Compare, for example, Isaiah 13.9ff. and 34:4ff., where the language of cataclysmic events clearly cannot be taken literally, as it refers to events within history – the fall of Babylon and the destruction of Edom.

14. For more detailed treatments of ecological concern from a Christian theological perspective, see R. Elsdon, *Green House Theology* (Monarch, 1992), and L. Osborn, *Guardians of Creation* (Apollos, 1993).

Conclusions

1. For an introduction to and survey of what is meant by post-modernism, see D. Lyon, *Postmodernity* (Open University Press, 1994).

2. Logical positivism was popularized in the English-speaking world by A. J. Ayer in *Language, Truth and Logic* (Gollancz, 1946).

3. See, as an example, D. M. MacKay, *The Clockwork Image: A Christian Perspective on Science* (IVP, 1974), pp. 40–47.

4. A. Peacocke, *God and the New Biology* (Dent & Sons, 1986), chs. 1 and 2.

5. For a short introduction to process theology, see C. Gunton, 'Process Theology's Concept of God', *Expository Times* 84 (1972–73), pp. 292–296; and L. Osborn, *Process Theology* (UCCF, 1985).

6. For a brief survey and critique of the thought of some influential process theologians, see N. L. Geisler and W. D. Watkins, 'Process Theology: A Survey and Appraisal', *Themelios* 12 (1986), pp. 15–22, and R. Gruenler, *The Inexhaustible God* (Baker Book House, 1983).

7. Gunton, 'Process Theology's Concept of God', pp. 295f.

8. *Ibid.*, p. 295.

9. Osborn, *Process Theology*, p. 31.

10. C. A. Russell, *The Earth, Humanity and God* (UCL Press, 1994), pp. 12–18.

11. See Psalm 19:1 ('glory' means the visible manifestation of the nature of God) and Romans 1:19–20.

12. This is implied in the ordered sequence of creation in Genesis 1 and passages such as Job 38 – 39.

13. Psalm 136:5; Proverbs 3:19–20; 8:22–31; Jeremiah 10:12.

14. J. Kepler, quoted in C. E. Hummel, *The Galileo Connection* (InterVarsity Press, USA, 1986), p. 57.

15. G. Zukav, *The Dancing Wu Li Masters* (Flamingo, 1989), p. 331.

16. S. Jaki, *Science and Creation* (Scottish Academic Press, 1974), pp. 192–218.

17. S. Mayer, *Values for a Sustainable Future* (UNED–UK 1994), p. 54.

18. J. Calvin, *Institutes of the Christian Religion*, 2.2.15 (Library of Christian Classics, vol. 20, SCM, 1961, pp. 273f.).

19. Bacon talks of God's 'two books' (the Bible and nature) in *The Advancement of Learning* (1605). See *The Works of Francis Bacon*, trans. and ed. J. Spedding, R. L. Ellis and D. D. Heath (Longmans, 1870).

20. See F. Bacon, *A New Instrument of Knowledge* in *The Works of Francis Bacon*.

21. Russell, *The Earth, Humanity and God*, p. 16.

22. J. Kepler, *Harmonice Mundi* (1618), Book 4, ch. 1. An English translation of Kepler's book is available in Great Books of the Western World, vol. 5 (Encyclopaedia Britannica Inc., 1952).

23. There is much debate about the exact meaning of two key words in Proverbs 8:22–31: v. 22 (possessed/created/gave birth to) and v. 30 (master worker/confidant/young child). However, two points are clear: wisdom existed in God long before the creation of the

heavens and the Earth; and wisdom was involved in the creative acts. (See the larger commentaries on Proverbs for detailed discussion of this passage.)

24. Quoted in C. Kaiser, *Creation and the History of Science* (Marshall Pickering, 1991), p. 127.

BIBLIOGRAPHY

Ayer, A. J. (1946), *Language, Truth and Logic*, London: Gollancz.

Bacon, F. (1870), *The Advancement of Learning* and *A New Instrument of Knowledge*, in *The Works of Francis Bacon*, trans. and ed. J. Spedding, R. L. Ellis and D. D. Heath, vols. 3–5, London: Longmans.

Birch, C., and J. B. Cobb (1981), *The Liberation of Life*, Cambridge: Cambridge University Press.

Birkhoff, G., and J. von Neuman (1936), 'The Logic of Quantum Mechanics', *Annals of Mathematics* 37.

Brooke, J. H. (1991), *Science and Religion: Some Historical Perspectives*, The Cambridge History of Science, Cambridge: Cambridge University Press.

Burnett, D. (1991), *The Dawning of the Pagan Moon*, Eastbourne: MARC.

Caddy, E. (1979), *Dawn of Change*, Forres: Findhorn Press.

Calvin, J. (1961), *Institutes of the Christian Religion*, Library of Christian Classics, vol. 20, London: SCM.

— (1965), *Commentary on Genesis*, Geneva series, trans. J. King, London: Banner of Truth.

Capra, F. (1982), *The Turning Point*, London: Flamingo.

— (1983), *The Tao of Physics*, London: Flamingo.

Chandler, R. (1989), *Understanding the New Age*, Milton Keynes: Word UK.

Clifton, R. K., and M. G. Regehr (1989), 'Capra on Eastern Mysticism and Modern Physics', *Science and Christian Belief* 1:57–66.

Cole, M., J. Graham, A. Higton and D. Lewis (1990), *What is the New Age?*, London: Hodder & Stoughton.

Coleman, J. A. (1966), *Relativity for the Layman*, Harmondsworth: Penguin.

Crowley, V. (1989), *Wicca: The Old Religion in a New Age*, Wellingborough: Aquarian Press.

Cuénot, C. (1965), *Teilhard de Chardin: A Biographical Study*, London: Burns & Oates.

Culver, R. B., and P. A. Ianna (1988), *Astrology: True or False?*, New York: Prometheus Books.

Dawkins, R. (1982), *The Extended Phenotype*, Oxford: Oxford University Press.

Doolittle, W. F. (1981), 'Is Nature Really Motherly?' *CoEvolution Quarterly* 29:58–62.

Elsdon, R. (1992), *Green House Theology*, Tunbridge Wells: Monarch.

Ferguson, M. (1982), *The Aquarian Conspiracy*, London: Paladin.

Feyerabend, P. K. (1975), *Against Method*, London: New Left Books.

Fordham, F. (1972), *An Introduction to Jung's Psychology*, Harmondsworth: Penguin.

Geisler, N. L., and W. D. Watkins (1986), 'Process Theology: A Survey and Appraisal', *Themelios* 12:15–22.

Gibbins, P. (1987), *Particles and Paradoxes*, Cambridge: Cambridge University Press.

Groothuis, D. (1990), *Revealing the New Age Jesus*, Leicester: Inter-Varsity Press.

Gruenler, P. (1983), *The Inexhaustible God*, Grand Rapids, MI: Baker Book House.

Gunton, C. (1972–73), 'Process Theology's Concept of God', *Expository Times* 84: 292–296.

Hanson, H., ed. (1970), *Teilhard Reassessed*, London: Darton, Longman & Todd.

Harré, R. (1985), *The Philosophies of Science: An Introductory Survey*, 2nd edn, Oxford: Oxford University Press.

Helm, P. (1987), *Objective Knowledge: A Christian Perspective*, Leicester: Inter-Varsity Press.

Hesse, M. (1963), *Models and Analogies in Science*, London: Sheed & Ward.

Hooykaas, R. (1972), *Religion and the Rise of Modern Science*, Edinburgh: Scottish Academic Press.

Houghton, J. (1995), *The Search for God: Can Science Help?*, Oxford: Lion.

Hummel, C. E. (1986), *The Galileo Connection*, Downers Grove, IL: InterVarsity Press.

Jaki, S. (1974), *Science and Creation*, Edinburgh: Scottish Academic Press.

Jantsch, E. (1979), *The Self-Organizing Universe*, Oxford: Pergamon.

Jones, D. G. (1969), *Teilhard de Chardin: An Analysis and Assessment*. London: Tyndale Press.

Jones, R. H. (1986), *Science and Mysticism*, London: Associated University Presses.

Kaiser, C. (1991), *Creation and the History of Science*, The History of Christian Theology, vol. 3, Basingstoke: Marshall Pickering.

Kelvin, Lord (William Thompson) (1901), 'Nineteenth Century Clouds over the Dynamical Theory of Heat and Light', *Philosophical Magazine* 2:1–40.

Kepler, J. (1952), *Harmonice Mundi*, English trans., Great Books of the Western World, vol. 5, New York: Encyclopaedia Britannica Inc.

Kinsbourne, M., ed. (1978), *Asymmetrical Function of the Brain*, Cambridge: Cambridge University Press.

Kirchner, J. (1990), 'Gaia Metaphor Unfalsifiable', *Nature* 345:470.

Kuhn, T. S. (1970), *The Structure of Scientific Revolutions*, 2nd edn, enlarged, Chicago: University of Chicago Press.

Lovelock, J. (1979), *Gaia: A New Look at Life on Earth*, Oxford: Oxford University Press.

— (1988), *The Ages of Gaia: A Biography of our Living Earth*, Oxford: Oxford University Press.

— (1990). 'Hands Up for the Gaia Hypothesis', *Nature* 344:100–102.

Lyon, D. (1994), *Postmodernity*, Concepts in the Social Sciences, Buckingham: Open University Press.

MacKay, D. M. (1974), *The Clockwork Image: A Christian Perspective on Science*, London: Inter-Varsity Press.

MacLaine, S. (1983), *Out on a Limb*, London: Elm Tree.

— (1986a), *Dancing in the Light*, New York: Bantam.

— (1986b), *It's All in the Playing*, New York: Bantam.

Mangalwadi, V. (1992), *In Search of Self: Beyond the New Age*, Sevenoaks: Spire.

Medawar, P. (1961), 'Critical Note', *Mind* 70:99.

Melton, G. (1990), *New Age Encyclopedia*, Detroit: Gale Research.

Meyerowitz, E. M. (1994), 'The Genetics of Flower Development', *Scientific American* 271:40–47.

Miller, E. (1990), *A Crash Course on the New Age Movement*, Eastbourne: Monarch.

Needham, J. (1959), 'Cosmologist of the Future', *New Statesman*, 7 November, pp. 632f.

Newton-Smith, W. H. (1986), *The Rationality of Science*, London: Routledge & Kegan Paul.

O'Hear, A. (1990), *An Introduction to the Philosophy of Science*, Oxford: Oxford University Press.

Ornstein, R. E. (1973), *The Psychology of Consciousness*, San Francisco: W. H. Freeman.

Ornstein, R. E., and R. E. Thompson (1985), *The Amazing Brain*, London: Chatto & Windus.

Osborn, L. (1985), *Process Theology*, Leicester: Universities and Colleges Christian Fellowship.

— (1992), *Angels of Light? The Challenge of the New Age*, London: Daybreak.

— (1993), *Guardians of Creation*, Leicester: Apollos.

Peacocke, A. R. (1979), *Creation and the World of Science*, Oxford: Clarendon Press.

— (1986), *God and the New Biology*, London: Dent & Sons.

Pedler, K. (1991), *The Quest for Gaia*, London: Paladin.

Pennick, N. (1989), *Practical Magic in the Northern Tradition*, Wellingborough: Aquarian Press.

Polkinghorne, J. C. (1986a), *One World*, London: SPCK.

— (1986b), *The Quantum World*, Harmondsworth: Penguin.

— (1994), *Quarks, Chaos and Christianity*, London: Triangle.

Popkin, R. H., and A. Stroll (1973), *Philosophy Made Simple*, London: W. H. Allen.

Rajneesh (1977), *I Am the Gate*, New York: Harper & Row.

Riddell, C. (1990), *The Findhorn Community*, Forres: Findhorn Press.

Robinson, H. W. (1947), *The Christian Doctrine of Man*, 3rd edn, Edinburgh: T. & T. Clark.

Roszak, T. (1969), *The Making of a Counter Culture*, Garden City, NY: Anchor Books.

Russell, C. A. (1985), *Cross-Currents: Interactions Between Science and Faith*, Leicester: Inter-Varsity Press.

— (1994), *The Earth, Humanity and God*, London: UCL Press.

Russell, P. (1982), *The Awakening Earth: The Global Brain*, London: Routledge & Kegan Paul.

Sheldrake, R. (1987), *A New Science of Life*, 2nd edn, London: Paladin.

— (1988), *The Presence of the Past*, London: Collins.

— (1991), *The Rebirth of Nature*, London: Rider.

— (1994), *Seven Experiments that could Change the World*, London: Fourth Estate.

Solages, B. de (1967), *Teilhard de Chardin*, Toulouse: Privat.

Storm, R. (1991), *In Search of Heaven on Earth*, London: Bloomsbury Publishing.

Talbot, M. (1981), *Mysticism and the New Physics*, London: Routledge & Kegan Paul.

— (1991), *The Holographic Universe*, London: Grafton.

Teilhard de Chardin, P. (1963), *The Phenomenon of Man*, London: Collins.

— (1964), *Le Milieu divin*, London: Fontana.

— (1965), *The Appearance of Man*, London: Collins.

— (1968a), *Letters to Léontine Zanta*, London: Collins.

— (1968b), *Writings in Time of War*, London: Collins.

Towers, B. (1966), *Teilhard de Chardin*, Atlanta, GA: John Knox Press.

Tudge, C. (1994), 'Make your own Morphic Resonance Kit', *New Scientist*, 26 March, p. 42.

Waddington, C. H. (1957), *The Strategy of the Genes*, London: Allen & Unwin.

Weiss, P. A. (1973), *Within the Gates of Science and Beyond*, New York: Hafner.

White, L. (1967), 'The Historic Roots of our Ecologic Crisis', *Science* 155:1203–1207.

Wildiers, N. M. (1968), *An Introduction to Teilhard de Chardin*, London: Collins.

Wolpert, L. (1984), 'A Matter of Fact or Fancy?', *The Guardian*, 11 January.

Zimmer, H. (1972), *Myths and Symbols in Indian Art and Civilisation*, Princeton, NJ: Princeton University Press.

Zukav, G. (1989), *The Dancing Wu Li Masters*, London: Flamingo.

INDEX

Confronting the New Age
The first book to tell you how to *confront* the New Age
DOUGLAS GROOTHUIS

The threat is growing. So not only do we need to understand the New Age, we need to stem the tide of this growing religious movement. Here's the first book that tells how.

You'll find all you need to know for:
Witnessing to New Age adherents
Identifying New Age influences in business seminars
Exposing New Age curriculum in our public schools
Discerning New Age influences in pop psychology, biofeedback therapy, visualization and New Age music

This book takes you a step beyond other books with its practical advice and sound suggestions.

230 pages   *Large Paperback*

Inter-Varsity Press

Revealing the New Age Jesus
Challenges to orthodox views of Christ

DOUGLAS GROOTHUIS

As the New Age movement gathers momentum throughout the West, Christians and non-Christians are encountering a variety of confusing ideas about Jesus Christ – both outside and inside the church.

Douglas Groothuis is already the author of two widely acclaimed books on the New Age movement. He now turns his attention to the identity of Jesus as proclaimed by the New Testament on the one hand and by leading New Age thinkers on the other. Which picture of Jesus carries the greatest historical credibility?

This compelling and readable book is an invaluable resource for Christians who wish to clarify their own understanding of Jesus and engage in intelligent dialogue with those influenced by New Age views.

264 pages   *Large paperback*

Inter-Varsity Press